ALL ARISE: CHUR(

Managing with Ministry Excellence

Yolanda —
May God bles
+ keep you

Pastor
Flippin

ALL ARISE: CHURCH ADMINISTRATION

Managing with Ministry Excellence

PEOPLE PUBLISHING is a trademark of LEDNEW Enterprise Inc.

www.LEDNEWEnterprise.com

Cover design by W. T. Dandridge, LEDNEW Marketing & Promotions Inc.

Dedications...

From: Dr. William E. Flippin, Sr.

To: My wife of almost 40 years, Mrs. Sylvia Taylor Flippin. Who, while I was administering and managing the church, she was holding it together at home.

From: Dr. James McWhorter

To: My wife Margaret of 41 years, for your unwavering love and devotion, and to my children, James III, Eric and Camille.

Managing with Ministry Excellence

Table of Contents

Managing with Ministry Excellence

Managing with Ministry Excellence

Managing with Ministry Excellence

Managing with Ministry Excellence

Introduction

More and more, the church of Jesus Christ is coming under attack from within and without. Some of the attacks against the Church are satanic, and others are dues to inadequate church admministration and management practices. In another instance, the church must be prepared to deal with these attacks-both spiritually and legally. Jesus said that the very gates of hell would not be able to prevail against the Church. The Church is the only force in the earth today holding back the onslaught of Satan and his army of fallen angels. The Church is already victorious and no weapon will ever be formed that can prosper. We must be able to disarm any weapon and destroy any obstacle in our way. Pastor Flippin has served as pastor of a small and large churches in the rural and city settings. What is the biggest difference in th two? The difference is the additional emotional weight. Paul explains this dynamic in II Corinthians 11:28. Dr. Gerald Brooks also helps us to understand that when you minister to more people, your emotional burden is multiplied.

Managing with Ministry Excellence

This book is a practical tool to help pastors with that extra weight. This book will assist church administrators, church managers, deacons, trustees, elders, ministers, church leaders and staff to effectively administer and manage the business of the local church. The Bible says, "My people are destroyed for the lack of knowledge" (Hosea 4:6). Some of the problems churches face today are due to ignorance of the law and basic business principles. This book is by no means a legal manuscript on church legality. However, it does provide practical help for churches to avoid many pit falls that they may be facing now.

Churches and church leaders are being held at a high level of accountability, now more than ever. It is extremely important that churches function and operate with integrity and accountability. This King's business requires haste and in all too many of our churches, time is out for business as usual. I trust you will find this book as useful and refreshing tool to assist you in being about our Father's business.

Dr. James MacWhorter,

Church Administrator

Managing with Ministry Excellence

Preface

It was hard to believe that I have been blessed with over thirty years of pastoral leadership. Initially, as a young pastor, I entered into this tremendous work very naïve as most will do. I concluded that everyone loved the Lord and were a part of the change to transform the world; and we ourselves are being conformed. My family raised me in what would have been a progressive church for that era. We had very professional printed materials i.e. bulletins, special programs, Christian Education materials, and Annual Church Vision and Budget. Our choirs were always robed and had a hymn book ready to be opened at any time. Because my parents never attended church business meetings, and due to the fact that I heard very little bickering and complaining among church leaders and members, I just assumed that all these church and ministry services were just the norm for most churches.

Few members of the church are absolutely clueless to the amount of energy, effort and enemies that will confront the advancement of the Kingdom. John Maxwell has often

---

Managing with Ministry Excellence

said and written that the early church of Acts people had no silver and gold, but they had power to make lame men walk. In the present culture, the church has silver and gold, but very little power to help anyone get up and walk. It is primarily of this reason (silver and gold) that churches have often become huge business enterprises and not soul saving stations.

Gerald Brooks of Plane, Texas writes that the book that has impacted his life and ministry is, "Why Smart People do Dumb Things" by Mortimer R. Feinberg. It is fascinating. Brooks says, to see leaders & churches cusp at what we'd consider greatness, and lose it all for dumb reasons. Not demanding church administration with excellence is a tragedy waiting to happen.

Indeed, the Bible does teach that all things must be done decently and in order. This is the reason that we stress and is the result of this book. Many of our churches have not understood 501c3 entities and the amount of paperwork, documentation, and financial scrutiny. All of this has further spilled over into the church. It must sadly be mentioned also

Managing with Ministry Excellence

that the moral and charater failures of clergy and church leaders has caused the church to be even more scrutinized under a microscope. Recently, the United States Congress was demanding financial records of several "mega-churches". The fear of some churches now is that any church, clergy, or ministry can be called into question.

We celebrate that Dr. Mac and I have combined experience of over 60 years working with churches and "church folk". We have seen the good, the bad, and the ugly. However, in summation, if and when the people of God are equipped and edified, all the hard work of church administration and management is worth it all.

Dr. William E. Flippin, Sr.,
Senior Pastor

Managing with Ministry Excellence

Managing with Ministry Excellence

A Church Administrator's Perspective

The ministry of Christ is a ministry of service. For over 32 years I have had the privilege and opportunity to serve as the church administrator of two large churches. The first was a Pentecostal church and the second and present one is a Baptist church. Although the polity differs from denomination to denomination, the core principles of church administration are the same. Although the leadership style of the senior pastor differs, their roles are the same.

In my first experience, the authority or power to govern the affairs of the local church resided solely with the pastor. Major administrative actions and decisions were approved by the pastor with little or no input from leaders or the membership. Not withstanding, a wise and prudent pastor will seek the advise, counsel and guidance of spiritual and knowledgeable church leaders and professionals. One of the advantages of this style of governance is that the vision and mission of the church can progress at a faster pace. Issues, plans, programs and directives do not have to always be discussed, debated and voted on before implementation can take place. The engrained culture is "the pastor said it, that settles it".

The disadvantage to this style of governance, if taken to the extreme, is that absolute power corrupts absolutely. I can't recount the number of times I've heard the scripture quoted and often out of context I must add, "Rebuke not an elder". As if to silence one for daring to ask an insightful or controversial question. If the pastor states "I am led of the Spirit" and makes a major decision plunder for example, the congregation suffers and his credibility gradually erodes. Too many plunders like this will render him ineffective and unable to garner support for other endeavors. This will also cause some members to leave the church.

In my present experience, the authority or power to govern the affairs of the local church resides with the congregation, at least for major actions and decisions. This form of governance is more democratic in nature. The pastor does have limited authority, but the final authority on matters pertaining to the life of the church rest with the congregation. In this instance, the pastor is not accountable to some diocese, bishop or headquarters, but only to the members that he or she serves.

The advantage to this style of governance is that "in the multitude of counsel, there is safety". All members of the church have an equal voice by their vote to affect the vision and mission of the church. One person, one vote; you can't get anymore democratic than this. I have observed that members, if they choose to, have a greater sense of ownership in the programs and activities put forth by the church. They are more apt to give their support than not. With their vote and depending on the issue at hand, they are saying "I'm all in" or "I'm opposed". A loyal and faithful member, even if opposed to an issue, will abide by the wishes of the majority.

A disadvantage I have observed to this style of governance is that the fulfillment of vision is often hampered or delayed. As I heard a deacon express once, "this church is like a big ship, it turns but ever so slowly". Meaningful and needed progress can take months or years to come to fruition. A simple act, for example, to change the name of a ministry is open for discussion, debate and a vote of the church body. A visionary pastor often feels frustrated and unfulfilled when vision tarries due slow or delayed inaction by church leaders.

Another disadvantage, or maybe it's a plus, is that only a remnant participate in the decisions making process. Thus major decisions are voted on by a small percentage of the congregation. This is indicative of the 80/20 rule. Twenty percent of people do 80% of the work in any organization.

An effective church administrator will grasp the leadership style of the pastor and at the same time learn and understand the culture of the church in which he or she serves. There will be those times when the two are not congruent. This knowledge and understanding will aid him

Managing with Ministry Excellence

or her tremendously in navigating around, over, under and through inevitable land mines.

The role of the church administrator is to always promote and communicate to leaders, staff and members the vision and directives of the Pastor. The church administrator is a member of the pastor's staff or team and is accountable to the pastor only. The pastor's staff functions for the sole purpose of assisting the pastor in serving the congregation, both leaders and members alike.

I conclude by saying that one form of church polity is not any better or any worse than any other. The aim or focus should be that God is gloried by our mission and purpose, the Great Commission is being fulfilled and the least and the lost are redeemed, reconciled, restored, and revived to a full life in service to others.

Dr. James McWhorter
Church Administrator

Managing with Ministry Excellence

Managing with Ministry Excellence

Administration and Management

The terms, church administration and church management, are usually used interchangeably. I like the definition of these two terms as stated in the book "*Mastering Church Management*" by Cousins, Anderson, and

> **Administration is managing the affairs of the church. Management is the process of getting things done through other people.**

DeKruyter. Don Cousins defines administration as "managing the affairs of a church effectively." Likewise he defines management as "the process of getting things done through other people." He goes on to say that, "Good managers have the ability to bring together the necessary people and resources to accomplish the group's goals."

We personally see effective church administrators as persons who can see the big picture, manage multiple tasks, understand and articulate the vision, enforce policies and procedures, and lead and manage church leaders to accomplish their goals and objectives.

21

Managing with Ministry Excellence

We also see effective managers as persons who are detail-oriented, able to delegate responsibility to others, follow-up in progress, manage multiple tasts, understand and articulate the vision, and bring the right people together to accomplish common goals and objectives.

Administration is the glue that holds the church together. It's like the mortar that holds bricks in place. A good biblical illustratrion of administration and management is Nehemiah and the rebuilding of the wall around Jerusalem. A careful study of this book will give valuable insight into how he strategized, organized, delegated, managed, and directed the rebuilding of the wall. Pastors who may not be strong administrators should surround themselves with persons that possess this gift. It will prevent a lot of unnecessary pain and heartache.

> **A well-managed church has a clear and understood purpose, knowledgeable servants, a workable strategy, financial integrity, and a well cared for "Main Street."**

Managing with Ministry Excellence

Don Cousins states that six "Signs of a Well-Managed Church" are:

1. A clearly defined purpose. There ought to be no mystery, no guesswork about why a particular church body exists. A three to five year strategic plan will always produce clear marching orders. Presently, our church has worked on leadership development, communication amg education strategies.

2. A widely understood purpose. In a well managed church, both the staff and congregation can articulate it's purpose. Each Sunday, we read our mission and vision statements as a part of the Sunday Worship experience.

3. Servants who understand their unique contrbution. In a well managed church, the individual players...know their role in making the church's purpose a reality. A good practice is to equip all leaders to write their personal vision statement.

*4. A strategy that works...*good management purposes that, refines, rethinks, scraps, and start overs—whatever it takes to hit upon a srategy that bears fruit.

Managing with Ministry Excellence

5. *Financial integrity.* Since money is a major part of church activities, the way it is raised, recorded, expended, and accounted for says so much about the management of the church. Annual, semi-annually or quarterly reports are critically important.

6. *A well-cared for "Main Street"*...a neat, clean, and attractive facility, especially those areas people pass through regularly. Trash, paper and other debris should, and does, drive some to insist that the church properties are always neat and attractive.

We recommend this book, "Mastering Church Management," as required reading for pastors, church administrators, and church leaders.

The Ground work for Every Pastor
The E's to an Excelling Ministry:

Effectiveness- In order to be effective in ministry all leaders must develop a collective consciousness towards to goals and vision of the church. One hinderance to a ministry from being effective is the unfortunate bond

Managing with Ministry Excellence

leaders will make with tradition and old mentalities. If a team does not have established goals and objectives it is possible that the team may be working hard and accomplishing tasks; but they fail to be effective in the work that is produced by the team. An effective church team will always stay focused on the process and will allow the results to manifest itself. When the process is maximized the results and the objectives will follow in the same manner. The modern environment can also influence the effectivness of the the team. All church leadership should desire to keep up with social trends and also the context they have been called to serve. One of the hardest things to do as an effective team is to be honest with themselves on how their thoughts and actions line up with the context they have been called to serve.

"For which of you, intending to build a tower, sitteth not down first, and countest the cost, whether he have sufficient to finish it? Lest haply, after he hath laid the foundation, and is not able to finish it, all that behold it begin to mock him, Saying, This man began to build, and was not able to finish. Or what king, going to make war against another king, sitteth not down first, and consulteth whether he is able with ten thousand to meet him that cometh against him with twenty thousand? Or else, while the other is yet a great way off, he sendeth an ambassage, and desireth conditions of peace." Luke 15:28-32

Managing with Ministry Excellence

Efficiency- What determines the longevity of a ministry will ultimatly be it's effenciency. The simplest method to an effective ministry is a great staff! When we elminate the burdens and stresses from one person and create a culture of team work, efficiency is possible. Many churches become stagnate because there is a small group of people trying to do everything. We have learned that effectivness focuses on the process and not solely the results. Efficiency evaluates the results based on the resources provided. It is only when a ministry can effectively measure their results that the determiniation of efficiency can be viewed. Great Pastors and administrators know how to effectively manage resources, but they also must be aware of managing waste in their ministry. In essence, efficiency is looking at what God has given you and asking yourself if you are making the best of your resources. Any great leader will communicate with their team the need to use resources and eliminate waste.

Managing with Ministry Excellence

Excellence- This element to ministry is the only element that comes from an intangible place. Excellence must become the mindset of your leaders, staff and people. The book of Philippians helps us to see this biblical standard in action. It is the thought that people will always choose their best and give their best in any situation they are called to serve. They become committed to giving attention to detail and maximizing the greatest potential of the situation. Because of this, the ministry will always display superior and above average service without compromising their moral values. Excellence is a mandate according to the scriptures and not just a consideration. Excellence is measured when effectivenss and efficient results are placed in retropsect to their highest potential.

Managing with Ministry Excellence

Managing with Ministry Excellence

Who Defines a Church: Bible or Government?
Definitions of a Church According to the Bible and the IRS!

In a sermon by Gerald Flury, he lays eight (8) biblical considerations for how a leader can define a church. These elements are biblically supported and should be evident throughout your ministry as a whole. In the course of this book and over the course of my ministry we have always held in high regard the type of ministry I believe God wants to see here on earth. We believe God wants us to be a people who are caring, committed and Christ Centered. There are many churches whose doors open and will ultimatly close because they do not demonstrate the biblical charateristics for what the church is suppose to look like here on earth (Acts 2:46). Many pastors and leaders believe that as long as they have a room, people, a preacher and an offering they have a church. Unfortunatly, none of these

29

Managing with Ministry Excellence

elements can build the foundation of a successful and growing church.

1. Be Sincere

All churches need to show and demonstrate a sense of genuine love for all of God's children. When people enter into your place of worship there should be a real sense of Christ's love that permeates the walls and the people gathered together. It is proven that more people have been brought into the body of Christ because of acts of love over any theological argument. To the same degree, many people have left the church because of the lack of love than any other argument. John 13:35 teaches us *"By this shall all men know that ye are my disciples, if ye have love one to another"*. Love is not something that can be easily explained or defined. However, a person knows when love is present and when it is not. We find it amazing how people will pass many other churches only to make their way to a church of their choice. The serious question should be asked, "why?" They feel overwhelmingly particular church is free of love.

Managing with Ministry Excellence

The best way to show love in the body of Christ is to simply acknowledge the presence of people. Bottom Line.

2. Be Considerate

As a church and as leaders and administrators, we must take the back seat. A true church will always put people before the brick and morter. Luke 6:31 helps us in saying, *"And as you would that men should do to you, do ye also to them likewise."* It has been proven in history that churches that glorify people and buildings will ultimatly fall by that same regard. As Pastors and Administrators we must remain conscious that all of our decisions are based on the needs and growth of the people we have been called to serve. Philippians 2:3 helps us with this concept as well; *"Let nothing be done through strife or vainglory; but in lowliness of mind let each esteem others better than themselves."* In the eternal triangle of Christianity, God is first, others are second, and self is last. You will know you are a great leader when your concern for others outweighs your concern for your self.

31

Managing with Ministry Excellence

3. Be Energetic

No one wants to attend a dead or boring church. When we say this we are not speaking of demonstrative expressions of faith. What we refer to is a sense of energy that permeates your ministry as a whole. As a pastor or administrator you should serve with such fervor that others get excited about the vision for the ministry as much as you do. In the Amplified Bible Romans 12:11 helps us with this: *"Never lag in zeal and in earnest endeavos; be aglow and burning with the Spirit, serving the Lord!"* As Christians we have a joy about life that others cannot take away! When we show that joy to others, they should feel the excitement we have about our faith! Always strive to keep a high level of energy at your church or ministry. This will help the people become excited as well about the great things that are happening in the body of Christ.

Managing with Ministry Excellence

4. Be Prayfully Patient

Get some camel knees- Pray! Pray! Pray! No spiritual battles can be won in the church until people, leaders in particular, get on their knees and pray. Developing a healthy prayer life as a leader will determine how healthy your ministry will become. I Timothy 2:1-3 helps us to see this charateristic in action; *"I exhort therefore, that, first of all, supplications, prayers, intercessions and giving of thanks, be made for all men; for kings, and for all that are in authority; that we may lead a quiet and peaceable life in all godliness and honesty. For this is good and acceptable in the sight of God our Savior"* Prayer becomes a powerful tool when leaders begin to use it. Many stresses, anxieties and battles will be won when leaders learn to pray through the storms. The greatest benefit of developing a healthy prayer life is that God will ultimatly become familiar with your voice over the voice of those who prey/pray against you!

---

5. Be Warm

Here we are not speaking about paying the heating bill in the winter. Rather I encourage all leaders to show a true level of hospitality. It is said that "people go to the church that is dearest to them... not the church that is nearest to them" This holds true on all levels of ministry. Hospitality becomes a by product of love. A simple card, phone call or even a text from a pastor, or church staff leader, to a new member can make the world of difference if that members stays with the ministry or not. Proverbs 18:24 says, *"A man that hath friends must show himself friendly..."* If no one else is to be hospitable in the church the Pastor and administration should lead by example. A healthy staff is one who is approachable and always willing to serve. One preacher wrote: "I am presently completing the second year of a three-year survey on the hospitality or lack of it in churches. To date, of the 195 churches I have visited, I was spoken to in only one by someone other than an official greeter...and that was to ask me to move my feet!"

6. Be Different

There should be a great distinction between the people of the world and the people in the church. As a church, pastor and administrator our lives should exemplify a level of integrity and humility. Matthew 5:39 helps us to see what a great leader should do in tough times; *"But I say unto you, That ye resist not evil: but whosoever shall smite thee on thy right cheek, turn him the other also"* It is unfortunate to say that in today's society you cannot see the distinction between the people of God and the people of the world. In order for churches and leaders to be effective this fact must change. Christians, especially leaders, should live a different kind of life. There is a different moral level and standard that we must strive towards in our daily living. We are not suggesting to live a falsified life of illusioned perfection. Rather we want each leader to strive for excellence and perfection in their living.

7. Be Understanding

The most powerful thing a leader can learn is the power of presence. As leaders we must learn how to be there for people and how to effectivly share good council. We must be able to empathize with our followers as well as those we have been called to lead with. Galations 6:2 helps us by teaching us to *"Bear ye one another's burden's, and so fulfil the law of Christ"*. Abraham Lincoln said, "I am sorry for the man who can't feel the whip when it is laid on the other man's back. As leaders we should have a heart for the pains of others. As leaders it is important that we understand the particular needs of those we have been called to serve. We must be sensitive to the fact that people don't need critics or people who will beat them up about their problems. Rather those we have been called to serve need us to be present with them in their time of need.

Managing with Ministry Excellence

8. Be One

The greatest characteristic that defines a church is the ability to be a team. It takes team work to make the dream work. As leaders and administrators we must be team players as well. A leader is only as strong as those they have been called to serve. It is said to note that many churches and church ministry leaders are not unified entities. There should always be the sense of "we" and "us" and not "me" and "my". No pastor, administrator or leader should be closed minded to the needs of the entire team. While your church may have its various leaders, ministries and projects understand that they all work for the common good of serving the entire body of Christ.

The CHURCH as Defined by the IRS

We have been able to analyze and acknowledge what the bible says regarding the definition of the church. However, all leaders must understand the legal elements of defining what your ministry is in the context of government and politics. To date there is no legal definition of a church used by the government. There have been numerous courts and bills designed in order to attempt what the makeup of a church should look like. Through out history there have been many contradicting opinions about what the church is and what it is not. In one court case, <u>Church of Eternal Life and Liberty, Inc. V. Commissioner, 86 T.C. 916.924 (1986),</u> the court described a church for tax purposes only as "a coherent group of individuals and families that join together to accomplish the religious purposes of mutually held beliefs."

The court stated that for legal purposes a church may start small (2 or more), but it will make attempts to grow beyond those numbers. In essence, a person who seeks to form a church for the purpose of only a select group of persons to become apart of it is not considered a church. A church, according to the government must always be striving for growth and community advancement. It is interesting to note that the governement does not define the church as the Body of Christ!

Should a Church Incorporate?

There is no law that states a church should or must incorporate. Incorporation is a legal matter, not a spiritual one. From a legal perspective, When is a Church a Church?

The IRS states, "Since beliefs and practices are so varied, IRS cannot define a Church, but resorts to a case-by-case approach to determine whether an organization is a Church."

A 1930 IRS news release listed the following guidelines for it's agents in

> The IRS uses 14 guidelines to determine if an organization is a church

determining if an organization is indeed a Church:

- A distinct legal existence
- A recognized creed and form of worship
- A definite and distinct ecclesiastical government
- A formal code of doctrine and discipline
- A distinct religious history

39

- A membership not associated with any other church or denomination
- A complete organization of ordained ministers ministering to their congregations
- Ordained ministers selected after completing prescribed courses of study
- A literature of it's own
- Established places of worship
- Regular congregations
- Regular religious services
- Sunday schools for the religious instruction of the young
- Schools for the preparation of its ministers

A *corporation* is a body of persons acting under a legal charter as a separate entity with its own rights, priveledges, and liabilities distinct from those of its individual members.

Incorporated – United into one body; formed into a legal business corporation

Unincorporated vs. Incorporated

Unincorporated Church (Court ruling) – The members of an unincorporated association (Church) are engaged in a joint enterprise, and negligence of each member in the prosecution of that enterprise is imputable (charged) to each and every member. Simply stated: Members are individually liable in civil action.

Incorporated Church – The law looks at an incorporated church as a single and separate entity and individual members are sheilded and excluded from civil action. In a civil matter, the assets of the corporation or church are subject to settle civil damages. The personal assets of the pastor and board of directors or trustees are not necessarily protected.

Managing with Ministry Excellence

To protect your pastor and board members, we strongly recommend the purchase of Board of Directors liability coverage. The cost may only be a few hundred dollars per year, but the cost far outweighs the risk.

We highly recommend that you become incorporated, if you have not already done so.

How to Incorporate Your Church

Secure the services of a competent attorney to:

1. File for name style with Secretary of State's Office

In an unincorporated church, each member is individually liable in civil action.

2. Prepare and file articles of Incorporation

3. Prepare your by-laws (or you can)

4. Obtain an Official Corporate Seal

5. Obtain tax-exempt recognition (number)

Articles of Incorporation

This is also known as "The Church's Birth Certificate." Articles of Incorporation contain the following information:

Managing with Ministry Excellence

1. Name and address of the corporation
2. Duration of the corporation (should be perpetual)
3. Purpose of the organization
4. Rules by which the organization shall be operated (general in nature)
5. Name of a registered agent.

Bylaws

Church Constitution: They contain the rules of the internal government of the Church. Bylaws should contain the following minimum provisions or rules that cover:

- Selection and requirements of the church membership
- Time and place of annual meeting
- Calling of special meetings
- Notice of the annual meeting
- Quorums
- Voting rights
- Selection, tenure, and removal of officers and directors

- Filling vacancies
- Responsibilities and powers of officers and directors.
- Methods of amending bylaws
- Purchase and conveyance of property
- Adopting rules for the order of church business meetings
- Ensuring compliance with certain state and federal regulations.

Minutes

This is the Voice of the corporation (Church). The minutes of the church should be kept in a secure place by the corporate secretary at the church (not at his/her home).

The minutes should contain the following:

1. The date, time, and place of the meeting

2. The type of meeting held (regular or special) , and a statement that the meeting was duly called and proper notice was given

3. The number of members present (in the case of board of directors meetings, the names should be included)

Managing with Ministry Excellence

4. A notation regarding the reading of the minutes of the most recent meeting

5. A detailed account of every action – from resolution to final action

6. A notation of the number of votes on each side of the issue

7. A verbatim transcrition of each approved resolution

There is a difference between incorportating and 501(c)(3) status

Over the past several years, courts have made a clear disinction regarding the difference between an incorporated church and a tax exempt church. There are many who believe the church should not be tax exempt. I have discovered biblical support for this. This interpretation of Section 508 (c)(1)(a) is established by case law, as ruled by the court in the case <u>Jack Lane Tayor Vs. Petitioner.</u> Below are some excerpts of the court's ruling.

(P)etitionaer contends that his donations to IBT are deductible because IBT is not a "corporation", but a "church"... He relies on section 508(c)(1) for suport for his position. Section 508(c)(1)(a) provides that churches, their integrated auxilaries, and conventions or accociations of churches are expected from the general rul of section 508(a). Section 508(a) provides that organizations described in section 501 (c) (3) and organized after October 9, 1969, are required to apply formally for recongnition of their tax-exempt status. Thus, section 508(c)(1) simply relieves churches from applying for a favorable determiniation letter regarding their exempt status as required by section 508(a). Nothing in section 508(c)(1) releives a church from having to meet the requirements of section 501(c)(3).

The court went one step further to rule that if the church does not have 501(c)(3) status the burden of proof for all donations is passed on to the donor to prove to the government that their gifts are deductible. Tax exemption is no longer automatically presumed for churches. While many non-profits are tax exempt, the status for tax exemption is not automatic.

Does getting 501(c)(3) status put the church under the control of the state?

Allow me to briefly tackle the theological aspect of this government status. There are many who will suggest that filing this status with the state subordinates the church to the government. As stated previously, these persons fail to seperate the Body of Christ from the organized church. There is no biblical stand that supports these claims; the claim of the church being subordinate or claim the church should be solely run by its leaders. The church is the Body of Christ. The Body of Christ is made of people; not entitites, associations or corporations. The bible teaches us as individual members live in peace and be subject to the authorities God has established. 1 Peter 2:13-17 says:

Submit yourselves to every ordinance of man for the Lord's sake: whether it be to the king, as supreme; Or unto governors, as unto them that are sent by him for the punishement of evildoers, and for the praise of them that do well. For so is the will of God, that with well doing ye may put to silence the ignorance of foolish men: as free, and not using your liberty for a cloak od maliciousness, but as servants of God. Honour all men. Love the brotherhood. Fear God. Honour the king.

The bible teaches us to submit ourselves to the ordinances of man. I see there is nothing in the section 501(c)(3) that makes us violate any of God's laws. It does not make us dilute the gospel of prevent us from proclaiming

47

Managing with Ministry Excellence

it. The only thing this status does, is raises the accountability of the church.

Managing with Ministry Excellence

HOW DO YOU INCORPORATE AS A CHURCH?

There are a number of churches in today's society who are not incorporated as legal entitites. We would highly recommend, if your church is not incorporated, regardless of how old the ministry is, to incorportate. There are benefits to incorporating and this process can save your church from future legal ramifications if needed. If a church is not incorporated, should a suit arise, the Pastor, each officers, staff & members can be personally held liable. If a church is incorporated, should a suit arise, only the church is responsible. At this point only the assets of the church are liable; not the Pastor, staff, leadership or members. In order to form a corporation, you must simply file your articles of incorporation with the state in which your church is represented. Once your articles have been filed with the Secretary of States Office, the state officially acknowledges your church as having formed as a corporation. Typically included in the articles to the state are: the name of the church, the purpose of the church, the address of the church, the original board members, and the name of the registering agent. We have noted that some churches actually add to their formal church name, incorporated. For instance, First Baptist Church, Inc,. Personally, we feel that this is not necessary. Make sure your paperwork is in order and not the name on your billboard or bulletin.

The Organizational Test

Just because you incorporate your church does not mean your ministry is tax exempt. Because of this, your member gifts cannot be considered tax exempt either. To go under tax exempt status, the IRS requires certain language be used and included in your articles of incorporation. This language is referred to as the organizational test requirements. The IRS requires this because it will substantiate that the ministry meets the exemption requirements of section 501(c)(3). This process can be long and strenuous for any church. It is my advice you seek legal help when going through this process; someone who specializes in this type of legal matter. Because the state does not provide the language, the church has to file articles of amendment and add the organizational test language. Without proper advise this can cause a church to spend extra time and money on the matter.

At minimum the language should consist of:

1. a purpose consistent with section 501 (c) (3); and

2. a dissolution clause stating that the remaining assets will be used exclusively for exempt purposes, such as charitable, religious, educational, and/or scientific.

Purpose Clause

The specific purpose for which the corporation is initially organized is to establish and oversee places of worship, conduct the work of evangelism worldwide, create departments necessary to support missionary activities, license and oversee ministers od the gospel, and to also engage in activities which are necessary, suitable to convenient for the accomplishement of that purpose, or which are incidental there to or connected therewith which are consistent with section 501 (c)(3) of the Internal Revenue Code. More will be said in chapter 7.

Managing with Ministry Excellence

Things to Consider when Considering your Ministry Relevent in the Eyes of the IRS

Do you have:

1. A school for the preparation of its ministers.

2. A distinct legal existence

3. Literature of its own.

4. A Sunday School for the religious instruction of the young.

5. A formal code of doctrine and discipline

6. Regular religious services.

7. A complete organization of ordained ministers.

8. A regular congregation.

9. A distinct religious history

10. Any other facts and circumstances that may bear upon the organization's claim for church status.

11. A recognized creed and form of worship

12. Ordained ministers selected after completing prescribed cources of study.

13. An established place of worship

14. A definite and distinct ecclecistical government

15. A definition of marriage that is legal and biblical.

Managing with Ministry Excellence

Organizational Integrity and Accountability

Financial integrity and accountability is an absolute necessity. If your church is to be held in high regards, by both the congregation and the general public, you must have high standards of integrity and accountability. No matter how good the pastor preaches or the choir sings, if church funds are not being properly handled or accounted for, you're headed for disaster. An annual church audit is recommended. You will need this for any future bank loans, etc. The process of an audit may be rather costly. It just makes good business sense.

> **High standards of integrity and accountability are absolute necessities.**

We are all stewards of God's resources including money. Simply stated, a steward is one who manages the affairs of another. God will hold us accountable for how we manage our money and the tithes and offerings given to His church by His people. Not only are

53

we accountable to God, but poor or wrong money management practices sets churches up for an unwanted audit by the Internal Revenue Service (IRS).

Definitions:

Integrity: honesty, sincerity, soundness, wholeness, completeness (Psalms 26:1, 41:12; Proverbs 20:7)

Accountability: Responsible, liable, answerable (Luke 16:1-2)

Promoting High Standards of Integrity

FISCAL YEAR – This is your church's financial year and it need not be the same as the calendar year. Your fiscal year helps you to better plan the allocation of your financial resources i.e. tithes, offerings, seasonal gifts, grant funding, ect. A fiscal year can be any time sequence you choose, however some commonly acceptable times are January-December, July-June, and October-September.

Managing with Ministry Excellence

BUDGET – This is the fiscal plan for your church expressed in dollars. Budgets should be firm, yet flexible.

> **Every member should have a spirit of ownership in meeting the church's budget**

This means it should be well thought-out and planned; yet there is room for unexpected spending needs. The budget process should include input from all key persons in leadership positions. This gives a true sense of ownership and team spirit, thus enabling leaders wholeheartedly to communicate and work to meet the church's annual budget.

Our experience is if the budget committee members are no rotated, it gives a false sense of control over the church finances. Also the member who remains on this important team for too long will always push and promote ministries that they support. Finally, a church budget committee must be saved, spiritual and seek to support and attend church activities. Too often, some budget committee members are only seen when they make their annual/quarterly persentations.

CHART OF ACCOUNTS – This is a detailed list of all church accounts with numerical categories to aid in proper bookeeping. This list will include, church assets, liabilities, fund balances, incomes and expenses. There should be designated accounts for investments. With computerized church accounting software, income and expenses are automatically posted to the proper chart of accounts categorized by using assigned account numbers. This is an efficient one-step process that alleviates mundane manual posting of church financial data.

CERTIFIED PUBLIC ACCOUNTANT (CPA) - This is a licensed professional certified by the state and matters of legal financial practices, financial accountability, tax law, financial review and audit. It is important to have an annual financial review and periodic audits of your financial records by an outside accounting firm. This will speak volumes about the overall integrity of the church. Again, let us stress, this

Managing with Ministry Excellence

person or firm should conduct an annual audit of all financial matters.

FOUNDATION STATEMENTS – These statements shape and define who your are as a church. We will discuss these statements in chapter 3, but you should review them often.

High standards of accountability: Who are you answerable to?

MEMBERSHIP – The congregation is holding the pastor, trustees, deacons, finance committee, and other persons, or groups charged with handling church funds accountable for how, when, and why church funds are used. Membership should be given

> **Keep your members informed and excited about giving.**

periodic and annual reports of church fiscal activities. After all, it's their money and the church is a family as well as a business therefore it is wise to keep your family members informed and excited about giving.

GENERAL PUBLIC- There is an old saying that you can do a thousand good things, but do one bad thing and everybody will remember that one bad thing. This is especially true when it comes to the church. You can feed the hungry, clothe the naked, open the blinded eyes, walk one water, but let there be one instance of money mismanagement and all your good deeds are lost.

GOD – We are stewards (trustees) over God's creation and we will give account to Him of how we've used or abused what has been entrusted to us. The word trustee implies "trusted". God's house is a house of prayer. It is sacred and sanctified and should be honored, respected and treated as such. This business of the church should measure up to the highest ethical and moral standards. God is watching (Luke 16: 1-2).

Form 1099 Requirements

If your church has given money to persons or contracted services for the rendering of the ministry your

Managing with Ministry Excellence

church is required to administer 1099 forms to the IRS. There have been various regulations and legalities churches have become unaware of. There are many churches who are not in compliance with these laws and requirements. These changes were added to the 2010 Health Care Act under subsection 9006 (b)(1) to ament the old IRC section Code Sec. 6041 (a). **It now mandates all churches, ministries, nonprofit organizations and businesses to issue a 1099-Misc form to any and all people, businesses and corporations for payments of $600.00 or more.**

The burden of 1099-Misc form

This new regulation now requires for churches to gather the name, address, and tax identification number of every person, corporation or business in order to do business with them by havign them fill out a form W-9

What happens if your church does not get a W-9 form from a vendor?

If your church/ministry does not get a W-9 from a vendor then the church will have to withhold a percentage of the payment and then submit the withholding to the IRS on a monthly basis using form 945. This can be a headache for churches. Think about having to withhold a part of your utility bill simply because the company did not give you the proper form. In essence, if the church does not withhold the tax, the church will have to pay the tax out of its own pocket. With the great expenses of many church budgets, imagine the weight of this expense. I believe this new requirement only opens churches to potential audits and ultimatly church closing do to failure of compliance. Some have refused to provide this information.

Who should receive a 1099-Misc from your church?

Under the new regulations, it no longer matters if the entity is a sole proprietor or corporation, everyone is required to get the form. I have provided a list of persons and companies that are required to receive this form if you do any business with them for more than $600 annually. It is important that the church minimally collects the individuals social security number so that these forms can be filed. (Examples listed on next page)

Note: When persons have performed services for our church and they failed to provide the information for us to complete the 1099, we complete it and send a copy to the person and the IRS. It then becomes the persons responsibility to report the income releaving the weight from the church.

What is to be done with the backup withholding?

An ideal situation would be if you have any backup withholding, you must file form 945 and turn it in by January 31st of the following year. For Example, on June 15th, 2010, Pastor Dave Jobs preaches at your ministry and does not provide a W-9. The church collects and offering of $1000. The church withholds $280 and gives Pastor Jobs a check for $720 and sends him on his way. By January 31st, 2011 the church must file the above mentioned form, sign it an mail it in to the IRS with the backup withholding.

1099-Mics Forms should be received from the following:

- Rental or church property
- Guest speakers, musicians, nursery workers and babysitters
- Coffee vendors
- Lawn care providers and landscapers
- Doctors and health care professionals
- Lawyers
- Cleaning and janitorial companies
- Media corporations
- Office maintenance
- Delivery services and postal services
- Drinking water companies
- Vending companies and goods
- Insurance agencies
- Books, and other publications.
- Renovation companies and beautification services
- Restaurants and catering providers
- Travel companies
- Cell, telephone and internet service providers.
- Utility companies
- Hotel and retreat centers
- Gasoline stations

- Church officers who are paid for duties related to their office. It is a normal practice, that church officers are never paid church funds.

Using Current Resources

There are various tools located on the internet and through the internet that will help your church to manage it's expenses to ensure the proper documentation is present each year as you prepare your taxes. Look in your local computer stores in order to find software that is simple to store and file this information for you. It is better to invest in this simple software for your ministry than run the risk of an audit by the government. A CPA can advise on this as well.

What happens if you don't file a form?

Under code section 6721, the IRS can impose penalties on failure to file, or correctly file information returns. The IRS usually finds out about filing issues through informers which it will pay with nontaxable fees. Penalties for filing issues can range from $50.00 to $250,000.00

When imposing a penalty, the IRS will send a NOTICE 972CG, which is titled NOTICE OF PROPOSED

CIVIL PENALTY. The IRS will give you 45 days for response to the notice and usually will waive the penalty if you are able to show that the incorrect filing was not intentional. Below is a list of sections of the law that relate to penalties for filing issues with form 1099-Misc:

301.6721-1, Failure to file timely correct information returns

301.6722-1, Failure to furnish timely correct payee statements

301.6723-1, Failure to comply timely with other information reporting requirements and;

301.6724-1, Reasonable cause

Form 1042S and nonresident alien guest speakers

While this information may not particularly pertain to your ministry it is good to have this information in your files in the event your ministry should grow to the position to invite international speakers to your ministry. By law, the church is required to withhold 30% of the offering paid to the nonresident alien, even if they have a tax payer identification number.Using form 8109, the chuch must pay the withheld tax. This withholding is due by the 15th of the following month of the visit by the guest speaker.

What happens when the speaker has no tax ID number?

In most cases, the guest speaker will not have a tax identification number. The church will then need to issue form 1042S copy A to the IRS and copy B to the foreign guest speaker by March 17th, of the following year after withholding the 30%. In addition to this, the church must also file form 1042 and send it to the IRS. Once the foreign guest speaker gets the 1042S, he/she must file form 1040NR with form W-7 attatched, to report the income in order to get a refund if any is due.

Foreign treaty exemptions

The United States has signed tax reduction treaties with various countries to ensure our citizens are not taxed too hight in other countries, and reciprocates to their citizens for income they earn while traveling there.

What if my church did not withhold?

It is possible that your church may not have witheld any funds from foreign nonresident aliens when paying an honorarium. According to IRS regulation, the church is techinically liable to pay that tax and send it in as though it withheld it, unless the foreign resident alien agrees to pay the necessary tax.

Guest Speakers and the W-9 form

Churches are to receive a W-9 form from any guest speaker before they step up to speak. A guest speaker may state that they would rather not give the church a W-9 because they may not want their social security number made public. In this case, the speaker can come to the church as a representaive of their ministry and give you a W-9 using the information from their ministry. If no W-9 if given in either case, the church will need to withhold a percentage for "backup withholding"

Managing with Ministry Excellence

Laying the Proper Foundation:
Who are you?

We know *whose* we are, but all too often, we don't know *who* we are. Nor can we or our congregation articulate who we are as a church to anyone we come in contact with. This is why the Foundational Statements are so very vital to your church. Foundational Statements shape and define who you are. Why you exist, what your focus for ministry is and those values you hold in high regards.

> **Foundational statements shape and define the who, why, what, and how of your church.**

The Church Growth Institute defines these foundationlal statements as 1) Statement of Purpose, 2) Statement of Objectives, 3)Statement of Vision, and 4) Statement of Core Values. Let's take a look at each one of these statements.

Managing with Ministry Excellence

Statement of Purpose

This is your mission statement, your purpose, and is the biblical reason your church exists.

1. It is biblical: a purpose statement should have it's foundation clearly in God's Word.

> **Your mission statement should be biblical, perpetual, and understandable.**

2. It is perpetual: At times a purpose statement may be restated to communicate to a new generation of people, but essentially it is unchanging.

3. It is understandable: A purpose statement must be communicated clearly so that people easily know what it means.

Statement of Objectives

An objective statement is an expanded version of a churches purpose statement. While the purpose statement may be short (25 words or less), the objective statement explains the purpose statement in greater detail.

1. It is special: Objectives detail how your particular church hopes to fulfill it's promise.

2. It is liberal: Objectives show the expanse of your purpose.

3. It is observable: Objectives may be seen in the churches basic structure and program.

Statement of Vision

A vision statement tells how you expect to work out the purpose statement in your church and ministry area. Characteristics of a vision statement are…

> **Your vision Statement should be perishable, practical, and achievable.**

1. It is perishable: Visions may be accomplished, forgotten, or lost.

2. It is practical: The vision must be relevant to your time, need, and place of ministry.

3. It is achievable: The vision must be big enough to challenge people but small enough to not discourage people.

Statement of Core Values

> **Your core values should be powerful, substantial, and crucial**

A value statement is a list of the basic concepts your church holds in high regard. For example, A congregation may place a high value on being a family church, or one that values tradition. Characteristics of a Value Statement are...

1. It's powerful: Values are hidden, controlling factors behind all decisions

2. It is substantial: Values are difficult to change

3. It is crucial: Value must be identified for effective ministry.

Managing with Ministry Excellence

Some examples of purpose or mission statements are :

"To know Christ and to make Him known."

"Meeting the needs of the whole person-Mind Body and Spirit"

"To fulfill the Great Commission of Christ through Christian Education, Evangilism and home of foreign missions."

Organizational Chart

To aid in laying the proper foundation for your church, develop an organizational chart. Once you have established your foundational statements, it will be easy to organize your church on paper. An organizational chart shows in detail how your church functions and will contain at least the following information. (See appendix for sample organizational chart):

- Chain of authority (command)
- How the church is governed
- Churches departmentalization

71

Managing with Ministry Excellence

- Horizontal and Vertical Relationships
- Placement of support ministries
- Flow of Information

The Church Constitution and By Laws

In our almost 60 years of collective ministry, we are still at awe with the number of churches who do not have a formal constitution or bylaws. What a church consititution and bylaws offer a church is the clear lay out of its structure, ideals, culture and principles by which to govern itself. Just like in government, without these to guide a church it will be hard to remain consistent and effective to understand the vision for the ministry. What the church constitution and by laws do is sets a standard to help a church measure their success and accomplishments of their purpose.

All churches need a governing document that is biblically based. **By definition, the constitution and bylaws is a document that contains the supreme law of the corporation and rules based on the Scriptures, by which the church will govern itself.** Because of this biblical standard, the church constitution and by laws are the most important document in your church's posession. So what is the difference between the church consitution and

Managing with Ministry Excellence

the church by laws? The constitution is considered to be the supreme law of the ministry. The by laws are simply the rules that are subject to the carrying out of the constitution.

What should be in your church bylaws?

It can become difficult for a church to determine what its bylaws are as opposed to the church's articles of incorporation. Some churches have a SOP (Standard Operating Procedures guide). One mistake many churches make is placing what should be bylaws in their articles of incorporation. We have seen churches who/that place their membership intake, discipline, doctrine and other detailed information in their articles of incorporation. The challenge in doing this is when the processes change so do the articles of incorporation with the state. It also involves a 4-step process: 1. A meeting with the board of directors, 2. The preparation of the articles for amendment, 3. Paying the state filing fee, and 4. Waiting for the approval.

Managing with Ministry Excellence

Any great leader or administrator should be one who is always striving to evolve the minstry into something great and greater. Because of the progressive church mindset I would recommend churches to amend their bylaws every two (2) years.

Reusing constitutions and bylaws

We are blessed to live in an age where technology can help us to pull resources and connect with others in order to help us with our projects. If you do choose to use technology in order to aid your progress be sure the information you pull is contemporary and relevant.

I know there are many young ministries who will simply look up another church's bylaws and constitution and post them as their own. If you decide to use another ministry as a model be sure to understand the essence of the information you are opting to use. Some of the church bylaws that are out there could be from decades ago! Your

---

Managing with Ministry Excellence

bylaws should be relevent to the context in which your ministry is serving.

Issues the church has to deal with today include: sexual misconduct, electronic privacy laws, zoning issues, background requirements and screening, techonology usage, liability insurance and much more. Be certain that your consititution and bylaws address the issues that are facing the church today. Know that the enemy will look for all types of legal ways in order to shut the doors of God's house. We would recommend if your bylaws have not been updated in some time, strive to make it a goal for completion within a years time.

What happens if your church does
not have bylaws or a constitution?

As Christians we believe it is not a good practice to take religious matters to the court system. However, we do live in a time where this moral standard is overlooked. I have come to realize that the court system would prefer to stay

Managing with Ministry Excellence

out of church legalities in order to save face to the church. In the event a matter should arise in your church, the court will always settle the case based on what is outlined in the constitution and bylaws of the church. Protect yourself. When these documents are not in place the court is then mandated to try the case according to the neutral principles of the law. Over the years, we have been called upon by courts and judges to provide assistance with interpreting some church constitutions and bylaws when the church is in conflict.

In cases where members were dismissed from the membership roles of the church, and the members have sued to be reinstated, the courts have rules that if the church has complied with its own constitution and bylaws, the court would have no jurisdiction. Wilkerson v. Battiste. 393. So.2d 195 (La. App. 1980)

I encourage you to make sure the wording used to determine membership, and guidelines for membership, are spelled out using very particular language. Some courts have intervened to make sure that the language is clear and not easily misconstrued. <u>Second Baptist Church v. Mount Zion Baptist Church, 466.P.2d 212 (Nev. 1970)</u>

8 Keys to Include in your Bylaws

We, and others have suggested the following items be placed in your church bylaws. These key things will protect you form the state and potential litigators. Including these basic elements will close any loopholes that could be present and create issues for you in the future.

1. Memership Requirements

As a ministry you have the decision to have official members or not to have members at all. It is recommended you have members. To list them as voting or non-voting members is at the descretion of the church.

Remember to include in your membership requirements a process for a person to complete in order to become an official member. All members should sign a covenant or agreement that says they will abide by the rules, creed and doctrines of the church. Potential members should also agree to be under the spiritual authority of the pastor and elders. Also included in the covenent should be a clause that states members are not entitled to a refund for their tithes and offerings or any other consideration that has been freely given to the church.

2. Accountability Board

This select group of people should consist of at least three persons who have no relation to the senior pastor. These persons should be in place to serve as counselors, advisors and accountability agents for the senior pastor. This small group of persons could have legal authority in the church. However, it may be best if they did not. In the event an accusation is made against the pastor the accountability board will be called in order to decide the matter, and if any, disciplanary action should be taken. This helps to meet the IRS requirements of having a way a pastor can be relieved from their duties in the event their actions are not conducive to the intergrity of the church.

3. Eccesiastical power of the Pastor

The bylaws need to state the pastor holds spiritual authority over the church. This authority allows the pastor veto power of the church board if need be. The senior pastor is responsible for the spiritual climate of the church and holds the final word concerning doctrine, practices and polity of the church. The Pastor serves as the chief overseer for all the ministry. In the event the Pastor and the board do not agree on a spiritual matter, the board will place the issue on the table for discussion at their next meeting. The Senior Pastor should be given enough time to prepare, in writing, their scriptural understanding for the issue.

4. Doctrines of the church and scripture

Including the doctrines in the bylaws simply says in the IRS's eye that the organization is a religious entity. Do not be afraid to include scripture in your bylaws when submitting to the state. Courts will often decide that if the matter cannot be resolved without going over doctrinal and religious issues of the church, then the courts have no jurisdiction over the matter. When this happens, the courts will call persons, like ourselves, who are experienced in such issues in order help the church bring about a resolution according to what is located in the doctrine, dogma, constitution and bylaws of the church.

5. Member privacy

As you will come to realize, many of your members will be concerned about their privacy. Assuring them their records are private and will be held in the strictest form of confidentiality will make them feel at ease. Your privacy clause should consist of the following:

a. The church vows to keep private all records concerning polity, doctrine, counseling, and information on membership.

b. The church vows not to disclose any records that may compromise information about a member's attendance, membership status, tithing or counseling records.

c. The church vows that no information about members will be released to any government without proper and valid documentation or valid supoena delivered by the proper government agency.

d. The church vows, if using internet and computer software, to install software that will aid in the protection of information.

6. Sexuality Clause

Going into the 21st century there are many states that continue to recognize same sex marriages or civil unions. In most cases, when a state recognizes something all organizations and corporation within that state must also recognize the statue unless there is a clear religious

Managing with Ministry Excellence

reason.Have a clause that your church, should it chose, does not recognize nor perform same sex unions. This will clear where you stand in the eyes of the community as well as clear your ministry in the courts. Also include in your bylaws a clause stating that your ministry leaders will go through an intensive sexual harassment workshop at least once a year. It would also be wise for all church leaders and staff to be trained on sexual harassment, "Safe Sanctuary" for children, and EEOC guidelines.

7. Standard of living clause

This clause is a standard of living that the church will suggest as the lifestyle for its members. In essence members are expected to uphold a standard of living consistent with the word of God. Any member who does not exemplify these standards could possibly be expelled by the pastor or the church membership. It was ruled by the Supreme Court in Jones v. Wolf, 443 U.S. 595 (1979) that to suspend or exclude from the Lord's Supper those found delinquent, is a matter concerning membership, solely under the control of the church, and that a member may have membership revoked if the pastor and/or church leaders deem it necessary.

8. Licensing and ordination requirements

As mentioned in "God's Order: Order in the Pulpit", all pastors should seek the counsel of the Holy Spirit when discerning the requirements for licensing and ordination. Recent IRS activities have questioned the legitimacy of mnisters for tax purposes. Many churches license and ordain ministers for the purpose of performing weddings and funerals to assist the senior pastor. However, for the special tax benefits that are given to ministers, the church bylaws need to state the legitimacy of the service conducted by the minister to the community. Here are a few suggestions:

1. At least 5 years of walking the Chrisitian Experience
2. At least 5 years of voluntary ministry relations at current or previous church.

3. Verbal acknowledgement and substantial studies of the New and Old Testament

4. The passing of a test or examination administered by the Board of Directors or council of the church on doctrine, polity and biblical interpretation.

Incorporation: Should we do it?

We spoke about this ealier, but we must stress an urgency here. You may be asking yourself, as a Pastor or administrator, should you incorporate? There are many other churches and pastors who have been challenged with this question. Consider this question instead, "Should I create a corporation for my church?" Always remember, from the bible's point of view, the church is the Body of Christ. Regardless of what the governement says, you cannot incorporate the Body of Christ.

There are some organizations who say you should not incorporate the church. Their belief is when you incorporate the church you make the church subordinate to the government. People who take this position do not have a clear definition what a corporation is. By definition **a corporation is an artificial entity (person) completely separate and distinct from its founders and members.**

We repeat from an earlier chapter, since an incorporated church is separate from its parishioners, the Body of Christ is not subordinate to the state. Simply put, an incorporated church permits the church to operate assets and policies and procedures without any one person, or members, being held liable. The church is able to re-create itself as often as it needs to when it is incorporated.

The Benefits of Incorporating

Church lawsuits have increased over 1,600% since 1992. With this being said, I recommend incorporating your church as a must! As a church, there are many benefits that come along with incorporating. The main benefit is LIMITED LEGAL LIABILITY. This benefit is commonly called the corporate veil. In simple terms, church assets, founders,

Managing with Ministry Excellence

officers, directors, and and other persons in leadership would be protected in the event someone should attempt to sue the church. In the event of being sued, attorneys will often go after the Pastor, administrator or directors. These persons are often seen as the ones personally responsible for the actions of the church.

If the church is incorporated, and the books are in order, the corporate status protects the pastor, administrator and directors from any personal responsibility. Be sure your records are in order!

Managing with Ministry Excellence

Managing with Ministry Excellence

Internal revenue Service (IRS) and the Church

Tax Exempt Status

Just because you're a church *does not* mean mean the Internal Revenue Service recognizes you as a tax-exempt organization. You must apply for and receive Exempt Status recognition from the IRS.

For our discussion, two types of exemption are **Individual** and **Group**.

Individual exempt status means your individual

> **The IRS determines if you qualify for exempt status**

church is recognized by IRS as a non-profit tax-exempt organization and is listed in Publication 78. *Group* exempt status means that the denomination you are a member of has a group exemption. All churches in the denomination come under this group exemption.

Who Determines if You Qualify for Exempt Status?

The IRS determines whether or not your organization qualifies for exempt status based primarily on the provisions within your organizing instrument, with special attention to the following items:

- The church is organized for exempt purposes, either religious, educational, and/or charitable activities.
- The church is operated exclusively for the exempt purposes outlined in your statement of purpose in the organizational instrument or the corporation
- No funds from the net earning (excess revenue) of the corporation will be distributed to private individuals or groups of individuals.
- The corporation will not become involved in significant lobbying or in otherwise attempting to influence legislation, or in the distribution of propaganda in such matters.
- The church itself will not participate in any political campaigning.

Managing with Ministry Excellence

- In the event of the dissolution of the corporation, the assets of the corporation (after the retirement of all indebtedness) shall go to another non-profit (501c3) organization.

IRS form 1023 is needed to apply for exempt status.

The Benefits of Applying for 501(c)(3) status

1. Exemption from federal income tax

2. Eligibility to receive tax-deductible, charitable contributions.

3. Exemption from certain employment taxes

4. Assurance to foundations and other grant-making institutions that are issuing grants or sponsorships to permitted beneficiaries.

5. State officials may grant exemption from state income and sales tax.

6. Counties approve property tax exemptions on propertty taxes

7. The U.S. Postal service offers reduced postal rates to certain organizations

8. Increased credibility within the congregation

9. IRS publication 78 will list your church as a legitimately organized, nonprofit, charitable organization, thus making it easy for anyone wanting to know your status.

Employer's Indentification Number

It is important to note the following:

- **Churches are required by law to apply for an EIN even if they do not have employees.** This may also apply to your state.

- **Possession of an EIN is not evidence of a tax-exempt status.**

Do NOT confuse the two. They are two different and distinct numbers that serve different purposes.

The EIN functions as the corporation social security number. You are legally bound to give your EIN upon request for legitimate reasons.

Examples :

1. Child Care Center

2. Summer Camp Program

3. Christian School

Managing with Ministry Excellence

4. 1099 Misc Income

5. Contribution Statement

IRS Form SS-4 is needed to apply for your EIN.

Unrelated Business Income

Churches are presumed to be nonprofit, tax exempt organizations,

> **Periodic bake sales, fish fries, and car washes are not taxable income.**

therefore their income is exempt from federal income taxes. However if a church receives "Unrelated Business Income" (UBI), they may be subject to federal income taxes and the filing of IRS Form 990-T.

If a church is having a bake sale to buy new communion utensils, or the youth are sponsoring a Saturday car wash to attend an annual youth retreat or the usher board is selling dinners to buy uniforms, these profits will be used for the benefit of the Church's mission (or purpose) as outlined in your Foundational statements. This is not considered Unrelated Business Income.

However if your church operates a retail for profit business catering to the general public, this is unrelated business income and is subject to federal income taxes. Examples of business churches have been engaged in:

- Restaurant or café
- Laundry/ Dry cleaners
- Grocery Stores
- Rental Property/ Apartments
- Charter buses
- Multi-level marketing

Another possibility could be if you were selling dinners in the fellowship hall and the public has accessibility, like at a Piccadilly Cafeteria. This can be construed as operating an unrelated business that is subject to federal income taxes.

Managing with Ministry Excellence

Common IRS forms To Be Filed by Churches

Form		Purpose
W-2	Wage and Tax Statement	For employers to report annual income and federal, state , and other withholdings
941	Employers Quarterly Federal Tax Return	For employers to report federal income and FICA taxes withheld from employee wages. This form is due quarterly
990-T	Exempt Organization Business Income Tax Return	For churches who engage in an unrelated trade or business.
1096	Annual Summary and Transmittal of U.S. Information Returns	Churches that issue form 1099to any persons must transmit copies of all such forms to the IRS with a

Managing with Ministry Excellence

		Form 1096
1099-INT	Statement for recipients of Interest Income	For churches paying interest in excess of $10 to any person must provide this form to the person on or before January 31st of each year.
1099 MISC.	Statement for receipt of Non-Employee Compensation	For churches to report compensation of $600 or more paid to guest speakers, evangelists, self-employed and other non-employees.

Managing with Ministry Excellence

Employee or Independent Contractors

Are church workers employees or independent contractors? In addition to full time

The vast Majority of church workers are employees and not self- employed or independent contractors

staff, how do you treat choir directors, musicians, part time custodians, and summer camp workers? The Internal Revue Service uses 20 factors to help determine independent contractor status. These factors are listed below:

1. Do you provide the worker with instructions as to when, where, and how the work is performed?

2. Did you train the worker in order to have the job performed correctly?

3. Are the worker's services a vital part of your company's organizations?

4. Is the person prevented from delegating work to others?

5. Is the worker prohibited from hiring supervisors and paying assistants?

6. Does the worker perform for you on a regular basis?

7. Do you set the hours of service for the worker?

Managing with Ministry Excellence

8. Does the person work full time for your company?

9. Does the worker perform duties on your company's premises?

10. Do you control the order and sequence of the work performed?

11. Do you require the workers to submit oral or written reports?

12. Do you pay the worker by the hour, week, or month?

13. Do you pay the worker's business and travel expenses?

14. Do you furnish tools or equipment for the worker?

15. Does the worker lack a "Significant investment" in tools, equipment and facilities?

16. Is the worker insulated from suffering a loss as a result of the activities performed for your company

17. Does the worker perform services solely for your firm?

18. Does the worker not make services available to the general public?

19. Do you have the right to discharge the worker at will?

20. Can the worker end the relationship without incurring any liability?

Managing with Ministry Excellence

*Note: Church officials and board members cannot and should not be paid for services rendered.

Social Security

Churches are required to withhold the social security tax (FICA) and Medicare tax from all employee wages. Likewise, the church is required to match both of these taxes for each employee and report it to the Internal Revenue Service. Most ministers are treated as self-employed for social security purposes and would pay the lesser SECA social security tax rate. The IRS also allows ordained clergy who serve full time on the staff to opt out of Social Security and receive a housing allowance. We will speak more about this matter later. Consult your accountant to see if you qualify for the SECA social security tax.

THE F. E. I. N.

What is the purpose of the F. E. I. N.?

The Federal Employer Identification Number is necessary to do business as an entity. To obtain an EIN number it simply involves filing the SS-4 form and submitting it to the IRS. The EIN is used for tax, banking and credit building purposes. This number is similar to a person's social security number. The church will use this number in the same aspect a person uses their social security number. The 3 predominant reasons for getting this number are:

1. To open a checking account

2. To establish credit

3. To file all pertinent tax and informational returns.

Does possession of an E. I. N. automatically assume tax exemption? NO.

The IRS and the Ordination and Licensing

The government has not had a major role in the process of ministers being licensed or ordained. What the government has been vocal on is how ministers will be treated for tax purposes. Unless a minister applied to enter the social security system, up until 1968, there were automatically exempt. Since then, congress has made it a requirement for all ministers to pay social security unless they apply to become exempt. This was done in order to prevent schemes from happening. There is an erroneous belief that ministers are exempt from all taxes, this is not true. Unless specific stipulations are made, all ministers are required to pay federal, income, and self-employed taxes, sales taxes, real estate taxes, and other taxes an average person pays.

There are, however, a few tax advantages to being an ordained minister who is employed by a legitimate church. If the ordained minister meets the conditions laid out by the IRS, the minister can take advantage of two benefits: 1. Housing allowance and 2. Self-employed tax exemption.

Sales Tax Exemption

This is an awesome benefit that is available in approx 35 states. It is unfortunate to say many churches do not take advantage of this exemption; primarily because they do not know it exist. On a daily basis, churches purchase products with a sales tax between 5%-8.5%. Most churches should not be paying this. I can assume no Pastor or administrator reading this book would refuse an 8% increase in their tithes and offerings. My personal recommendation is all churches take advantage of this simple exemption. Note that all purchases or lease agreements your church makes will qualify to receive this exemption. As long as the item is used for ministry purposes.

A great example of this would be the purchase of a new church bus. Let's assume you decide to purchase a church van for $17,500.00. After sales taxes are tacked on the total price of the vehicle will be $18,550.00 If your church has applied for this exemption you will save $1,050.00! This is a great savings that could be used to support other aspects of your ministry.

Managing with Ministry Excellence

How to apply for sales tax exemption

Applying for a sales tax exemption is not as difficult as applying for 501 (c)(3) status. However, many states require a church to have 501(c)(3) status before applying for sales tax exemption. In most states this is handled by the department of revenue. A word of caution is to ensure your paperwork is consistent with other paperwork you have filed with other government agencies; as they do have a tendency to cross reference.

Managing with Ministry Excellence

Managing with Ministry Excellence

More About the Internal Revenue Service

Loans to members

Since the church is not in the business of loaning money and this is a practice reserved for banks and other lending institutions, churches should have a clearly defined policy of not lending church funds. The churches non-profit, tax-exempt status precludes it from lending church funds. The church can assist a member with a benevolent need provided there are no strings attached and repayment is not a condition for extending the benevolent aid. The church should have a clear and precise policy for managing a benevolent fund.

Pastor's Anniversary

Most churches have an annual pastor's anniversary or appreciation. The question arises, "is this a gift or income to the pastor?" Historically the Pastor's Anniversary is a major event in the life of the church, often climaxing after several months of planning, preparation, and fundraising. A

Managing with Ministry Excellence

chairperson is appointed, usually by the pastor, to spearhead the affair, banners are hung, announcements are made, other guest churches and ministers are invited, a dinner or banquet is held and all is culminated on a particular Sunday, with members asked to give a certain amount.

The answer to the above question is that all funds raised for the pastor's anniversary is income to the pastor and should be reported as such. Funds that are openly solicited are not a gift but income. Even if checks are made payable to the pastor or money given directly to him, it is still income to the pastor.

A gift must be spontaneous and unsolicited. Case in point: Sister Heart Ache was spiritually blessed and deeply touched by the pastor's sermon. After the benediction, she went up to the pastor as he was shaking hands and expressed to him how the sermon had helped her spiritually. She shook his hand and gave him $20. This was a gift that was spontaneous and unsolicited.

Managing with Ministry Excellence

Political Involvement

Churches are prohibited by the Internal Revenue Code from participating and contributing directly or indirectly to any political campaign. Churches and specifically ministers should not use the pulpit to:

- Endorse a particular candidate
- Publish a candidate's statement in the church bulletin, newsletter, or flyers
- Raise funds or receive an offering for a candidate
- Use church funds to make a campaign contribution or pay campaign expenses
- Allow a candidate to address the congregation to solicit voters. (Remember equal time and separation of church and state)

Churches can encourage its members to vote and sponsor voter registration drives, however, not with the intent of supporting a particular candidate or party.

Pastoral Love Offerings

It is common that churches want to bless their pastor. In most churches this is executed by using special days to take up love offerings. These offerings are used to show affection, respect, and admiration to the pastor. In some cases this is done at will in order to surprise pastors with a gift of love. The church and its members consider this a gift and not a part of the pastor's salary. Regardless of the intent, love offerings **ARE NOT** to be executed from the pastor's gross income.

Some churches consider love offerings as gifts and not gross income that must be reported to the IRS. Part of this misconception is because section 102 of the Internal Revenue Code which states gifts are not taxable. Under section 102 (a) a gift "must proceed from a 'detached and disinterested generosity,'...'out of affection, respect, admiration, charity or like impulses.'" <u>Commissioner v. Duberstein, 363 U.S. 278.285 (1960)</u>

Managing with Ministry Excellence

Though this code allows a person to exclude gifts from gross income, it is difficult for many churches to do this in a way that is not taxable. Here are our recommendations to follow:

1. All love offerings cannot be mentioned as a part of a pastor's compensation package or contract.
2. The church should use special envelopes for the Pastor's love offering.

   a. Having a separate envelope shows it is an individual gift of affection or admiration.

   b. The gift is considered tax deductible if the church or Pastor should report it as income.

   c. Parishioners will know their gifts are not tax deductible because these gifts will go directly to the pastor.

   d. Using a regular church envelope makes the gift tax deductible for the giver and taxable to the pastor.
3. It should be stated from the pulpit that gifts given to pastor are not to compensate for his/her service; but rather what the pastor means to the giver individually

Are there other ways to give?

If a pastor has taken advantage of a housing allowance and become exempt from self-employment taxes, most of their income can be exempt from taxation. The church can receive the love offering and give it to the pastor without any withholding. The pastor will then include this on the W-2. This could place the pastor in position to no or lower taxation. What this also means is the church will not need to get special envelopes done. Another option, some churches use are for occasions like birthdays, Christmas or anniversaries, the church can create a deferred housing allowance which will grow tax free for the pastor until it is cashed out.

Don't retire a broke preacher!

It is sad to say many preachers retire without proper financial planning for sustaining their lives outside of pastoring. Many pastors, either worked little or not at all on a secular job. Since they file for self-employed tax exemption they do not receive any social security benefits.

Managing with Ministry Excellence

There are three things I would recommend Pastor's do to ensure they do not retire broke:

1. Ensure the pastor gets at least 10 years of secular employment to qualify for social security. *The minister must make a minimum of $4,480.00 per year in secular employment to receive 4 credits towards social security.

2. Consult your financial advisor and create a simple Roth IRA

3. Take full advantage of the deferred housing allowance.

Some other recommendations for retirement

As a Pastor you must be savvy with investments. Use your money wisely and do things in order to make it grow! We would recommend you to use some of your saved taxes to invest them in an asset of wise choice. We would also recommend all pastors to look into ministry and business opportunities that produce passive and various forms of income.

How to use the Deferred Housing Allowance: What is it and why is it an attractive option?

In simplest terms the deferred housing allowance will allow a pastor to build equity in a current home or future home the pastor will purchase. The deferred housing allowance can also be used for retirement. It is unfortunate to note a number of pastors who do not own a home. Many pastor's rent properties or live in a parsonage. Those who do own would love to earn extra equity!

In order to execute a deferred housing allowance plan, the church and pastor reach an agreement the church will deposit a set amount, monthly, in an interest bearing account that will grow tax free for the pastor. A key to this plan is the funds must remain in full control of the church and can only be dispersed to the pastor according to the written contract. The church has the option to deposit weekly, monthly or on special occasions where love offerings are taken up. These gifts will be tax deductible to the givers.

Why the deferred housing allowance? The funds saved can be distributed to the pastor in one lump sum or over time. As long as the church controls the plan, the pastor can claim the allowance exclusions on the distributions. If the pastor is self-employment exempt, they will benefit from additional tax savings.

Honorariums

An honorarium by definition is a payment to a professional person for services on which no fee is set. Guest speakers, evangelists, revivalists, and other clergy persons do not usually have a set fee for ministering God's Word. For most, this would be unethical. However this trend is changing. Some clergy and musicians have contracts/agreements to complete before they accept a ministry opportunity. This can include, hotel accommodations, flight arrangements and product sales agreements. The amount a guest minister is compensated is usually left to the discretion of the pastor.

A guest speaker (or singer) should be asked to complete IRS Form W-9 "Request for Taxpayer Identification Number and Certification." Be sure they fill in their social security number, sign, and date it. Some guest speakers prefer to use their ministry name, in this case, be sure they give you their Employer Identification Number. If a guest speaker refuses to complete IRS Form W-9 you are required by law to withhold "Backup Withholding" at the current rate and report this tax to the Internal Revenue Service on IRS Form 945.

Again we repeat, any guest speaker the church compensates $600 or more in any year should be given IRS Form 1099-MISC by January 31st of the next year. Case in Point: Evangelist Swing Lowe spoke for your church in February, July, And November 1997. He receives an honorarium of $200 each time. Evangelist Love completed form W-9 in February and his total honorarium was $600 dollars for 1997. On or before January 31st, 1998 The church will mail Evangelist Love IRS Form 1099-Misc. Noting in Box 7, $600 of Nonemployee Compensation.

Interest Payments

Some churches have been acquired or purchased through a church bond program. A church bond program is where a church issues bonds through a bond company for sale to anyone. The money received from the sale of bonds goes to the church to acquire its property. The church agrees to pay bondholders back, principle plus interest, over a period of time, usually 10, 15, or 20 years. Bonds usually mature or come due every six months, meaning the church must have these funds available in a specified bank account to pay bondholders at maturity.

The interest paid by the church to the bondholder is interest income to the bondholder. On or before January 31st of each year, the church must issue each bond holder

115

whose bond matured the previous year an IRS Form 1099-INT, "Interest Income Statement." This form is issued on all interest paid by the church of $10 or more.

Contributions of $250 or More

Cancelled checks are no longer absolute proof of a contribution (1993 tax bill). For contribution of $250 or more, churches must now issue a receipt to the donor (member, friend, or visitor.) The receipt must be issued at the time the contribution is made (within a few days) and not several months later. A separate receipt should be issued for each gift or contribution. Case in Point: You have a faithful member who tithes consistently. He is paid every two weeks and his gift is $300. At the end of the year, he would receive 26 receipts of $300 each from the church for his tax records.

Contribution Envelopes

Church members and attendees should be encouraged to use contribution envelops, especially if cash is given. The use of envelopes provides an easy way to post contributions to each member's name by the bookkeeper or financial secretary. Envelopes also deter people from removing loose cash from the offering tray. The finance or count committee should always verify that the amount written on the envelope is the correct amount in the envelope.

Contribution envelopes should be kept in a safe and secure place in the church for at least three years before being discarded. This is important for future verification if needed by an individual donor and for IRS purposes. Annually, many churches will provide a member their statement of giving for the year.

Housing Allowance

Current laws and codes allows ministers to have a housing allowance. The term "housing allowance" does not mean a type of stipend or pay from the church. What this means through the eyes of the IRS is an allowance of tax deductions equal to the actual cost the minister incurred for providing a home for themselves and their family.

How do you calculate the housing allowance.

There are three scenarios a minister must use to calculate their housing allowance. Using the following three scenarios, a minister must use the lowest of the three on their W-2.

THE HOUSING ALLOWANCE EXPLAINED HOUSING ALLOWANCE CLARIFICATION ACT OF 2002

STEP 1

On January 1st, 2011 you calculate the actual home expenses for 2010

STEP 2

On January 1st, 2011 you estimate home expenses for 2011

STEP 3

On January 1st of every year, you calculate the rental value of your home

The grand total of each of the above are entered into the housing allowance statement allowance statement, signed and given to the church treasurer to be stored in the corporate records kit.

How to create the housing allowance?

The first step for creating the housing allowance, a board meeting must be called in order to adopt the plan for the minister. If the church has more than one staff pastor, a plan will have to be developed for each one. The resolution from the board must contain the following:

1. The date the board meets. This is because the plan cannot be retroactive.
2. A quorum must be in attendance.
3. The housing allowance terms should be permanent unless revoked
4. The pastor's name must be clearly stated in the housing plan
5. The board must require a housing allowance statement from the pastor on the 15th of January

How does a pastor qualify for a housing allowance?

There are stipulations according to the IRS that qualify a pastor to receive a housing allowance. The first qualification is the minister must be ordained or licensed clergy of a particular church. The minister must also perform certain functions to be considered. These would include:

1. Performing sacerdotal functions

2. Conducting religious worship

3. Holding a leadership position where they control, conduct, and maintain religious organizations, boards or other religious bodies.

4. Be active in an administration duty such as teaching or instructing at a theological seminary, as long as the institution is under control of the church.

5. Performing the ordinary duties of a minister as an employee of the United States, a state, political subdivision or District of Columbia (with the exception of Chaplain in the Armed Forces)

The Basics:

1. Be ordained by church requirements
2. Have a housing allowance plan clearly filed in the church's approved minutes
3. Receive some type of pay for the purpose of performing a service related to ministry.

After looking at these stipulations, all pastors and staff pastors will qualify for the allowance. Likewise, most worship leaders, youth & children's pastors and other ministers may qualify.

Managing with Ministry Excellence

Managing with Ministry Excellence

Financial Operations

Handling of Funds

To ensure the financial integrity of your church and to maintain high standards of integrity and accountability, you will need to have clear and precise policies and procedures for handling church funds. In addition, a job description is needed for all individual handling church funds. You cannot in truth and fairness hold someone accountable for what you expect or require them to do. Job descriptions also help keep people on task and from straying in areas assigned to others.

TRANSPORTATION

After the funds have been collected in the worship service, they should be transported to a safe and secure place in the church immediately. If possible, it should be by the shortest route. Transporting funds a long distance, to another building, or up and down stairs is a serious security risk. It may be worth taking the added precautions of having a few deacons posted along the transporting route to insure the path is clear or hire an off duty law enforcement officer to escort the money handlers.

WHEN TO COUNT

Funds should be counted as soon as possible. Some may choose to count immediately after the offering is taken and others at the conclusion of the worship service. Some pastors may require that church business be taken care of after the benediction so that all can be spiritually fed. If funds are not counted immediately, that should be locked in a safe and secure place, preferably a fireproof safe. Counting should occur in a location away from the public view and without unnecessary interruption. A minimum of two persons should be in the count room at all times. Be sure to have all the necessary tools you need – calculator, money straps, coin rollers, rubber bands, count sheets, tape, pens, stamp pad, deposit stamp, and deposit slips. Persons in the church with banking backgrounds would be an asset to serve on this committee. They count money each day and would know the

Managing with Ministry Excellence

latest machines, technology and procedures not to make this a tedious task.

Avoiding Impropriety

Things are not always as they appear. To protect those who are responsible for counting church funds from false accusations and unnecessary or unwanted scrutiny, a standard practice may be for individuals to serve on a rotating basis. Since an individuals' giving should be kept confidential, rotating counters would avoid unnecessary curiosity. Also, if funds are counted during the worship services, by rotating counters, they will only miss a few worship services per year. Your church accountant will be able to provide the best practices.

Required Financial Committees and Officers

Count Committee- Responsible for counting all church funds and preparing funds for bank deposit. Funds should be strapped according to banking standards. If needed, check with your churches banker regarding this procedure. Members should serve on a rotating basis.

Budget Committee- we earlier mentioned that they are responsible for preparing the church's annual fiscal budget including department boards, and auxiliaries. Depending on the church organization structure, the annual budget should be adopted by the board of trustees or congregation as stated in the bylaws.

Finance Committee- responsible for overseeing the receipt and disbursement of church funds and helping to keep the church's financial operations on or under budget. The committee may be part of the Trustee Board. The committee should make periodic financial reports available, and submit a financial report to all church leaders, including the Senior Pastor. We have come across some churches where the leaders adamantly refuse to give the Pastor a report of the offering receipts. They maintain the Pastor should only handle spiritual matters and that the designated leaders will handle the temporal (financial). There will eventually be a collision. Everything the church involves itself in is "spiritual and biblical".

Audit Committee- Responsible for auditing the financial records of the church on an annual basis, preparing the church's annual report. They may solicit the service of a CPA.

Treasurer- responsible for the receipt, safekeeping, and disbursement or church funds. Should be bonded by the church's insurance provider.

Financial Secretary/Bookkeeper/Business Manager – responsible for the handling and care of church envelopes, posting, recording or contributions, preparing checks, and handling accounts payable and receivable. Depending on the size of your church, you may choose to separate these positions.

Posting Financial Data

Check Writing- checks should be posted or recorded to the appropriate ledger sheet at the time the check is written. It is a good practice to set aside a certain day each week to pay all bills for that week. Any unexpected or emergency checks can be written as the need arises. No blank checks should be issued—if lost they can be cashed.

Computer Software is available that will allow you to print checks and the payee is automatically posted to the proper account category using the account numbers in your chart of accounts.

Membership Contributions – Contributions should be posted to the donor's file within a few days of receiving the gift. For any contribution of $250 or more, a receipt should be mailed and received by the donor by the end of the week. This will help to ensure integrity and accountability in the mind of the donor. No cash is ever to be given in this situation.

Contributions should be posted from the offering envelope, which includes checks too. If a check is placed in the offering tray, but not in an envelope, the count committee should take time to make an envelope to the donor. Remember that envelopes are the church's record for any future verification or IRS inquiry.

COUNT SHEET

A count sheet (or tabulation sheet) should be used to account for all income. This is a simple form used by the Count Committee and copies can be made as more forms are needed. The form should be signed by the count committee to verify that the receipts are true and accurate. You may want to include a copy of your count sheet with your bank deposit, especially if you are using the night deposit. Bank tellers are human and they do make mistakes. See appendix for a sample count sheet.

Internal Disbursement Procedures

Who is responsible for disbursing church funds? Well, no one individual should have carte blanche to approve church expenditures, prepare church checks, and sign church checks especially for non-budgetary expenses. The business manager financial secretary prepares the checks, and the business manager signs the checks. This could be the responsibility of the trustees as well. There should be no problem for the business manager or financial secretary to prepare checks for budgetary items. Some expenditures are routine, namely, the utilities, mortgage note, payroll, and loan payments.

We strongly recommend that in most instances, two signatures be required on church checks. There may be a few exceptions to this rule, say for instance, a separate payroll checking account. Also, any checks marked "void" should be kept by attaching them to the check stub with the cancelled checks.

Managing with Ministry Excellence

Checks should be written and mailed when the funds are in the bank. Avoid writing "FAITH CHECKS". That is writing checks and trying to raise funds to deposit before the check hits your bank. The church does not want to be known as a church whose checks bounce. Do not allow blank checks to leave the church. On rare occasions, someone may need to carry a check to make a purchase. However, the business manager should write the date, name of payee, and write what the check is for. The person should return the receipt so the actual amount of the check can be posted.

Payments to vendors should be by an invoice. If an invoice is lost or misplaced, have the vendor fax you a copy of your current statement. (YOU NEED A FAX MACHINE.) Be sure to write a memo on the check; both the account number and what the check is for.

Managing with Ministry Excellence

Managing with Ministry Excellence

More Financial Data

PETTY CASH FUND

This is a fund for incidental expenses and not for major purchases or church supplies that are routinely ordered. For instance, the secretary needs a ream of yellow paper or a phone message book. Rather than issuing a check for this small amount, a few dollars can be obtained from petty cash fund.

The church should set a written limit on petty cash. A reasonable maximum limit on petty cash expenses could be for purchases $20 or less. The church should budget an amount for petty cash on a monthly basis say $200 per month. At the end of each month, the petty cash fund is reconciled and brought back up to the $200 per-month limit. If the petty cash fund is exhausted before the month ends, the matter should be brought to the attention of the church leadership or business manager for an emergency allocation if needed, or a "hold" should be placed on the fund. It may mean increasing the petty cash limit if funds are exhausted too often.

Whenever petty cash funds are disbursed , the recipient should sign for cash receipt (use of a petty cash received slip) and return the vendor receipt and any change. This should equal the actually amount received.

Petty cash receipt books can be obtained from your local office supply company.

BANK DEPOSITS

Church funds should be deposited the same day they're received, if possible. If not the same day, then certainly the next banking day. This will allow for checks to clear your account, thus avoiding return items. Deposit slips should be made out in duplicate, with the original going to the bank and you keeping the copy. Remember, you may want to include a copy of the count sheet, especially for large deposits. Checks should be listed on the deposit slip for small deposits and adding machine tape attached for large check deposits. Always be sure to stamp the back of each check with the church's bank deposit stamp along with stamping strapped cash and rolled coins.

Depositing Church Funds

Allow us to stress again, church funds should be deposited in the bank as soon as possible. For security reasons, funds should be transported to the bank in a locked moneybag by at least two persons. If possible, use the banks night deposit box. Another security precaution would be to use two vehicles, one following the driver with the money to the bank. Try not to leave anything to chance- a person's life is worth more than a few hundred or few thousand dollars. Another precaution is the services of a securities service. Remember to "watch AND pray." There are paid pick up services that can be considered as well.

RECONCILE BANK STATEMENTS

Monthly bank statements should be reconciled if possible upon receipt or within 2-3 days at the longest. Bank statements should be reconciled at the end of each month. Any errors or mistakes should be corrected and if needed, brought to the bank attention immediately. Reconciliation allows the church to correct and discrepancies before they get out of control and verifies the actual cash the church has in the bank for a particular timeframe.

Credit Cards

Corporate credit cards can be a needed asset if handled properly and a

Church credit cards should be used for church business only.

nightmare if abused. The church will need to establish a board policy for credit card use by it's employees. We strongly recommend that the use of the church's credit card be for church business only and only for personal use in extreme emergencies. Ideally, employees should have their own credit card for personal use. This totally avoids the use of the church's credit card. Furthermore, the church leadership may choose to define what constitutes church use by employees. Here are some examples:

- Approved travel/hotel/meals by officers/staff
- Guest travel/hotel/meals
- Church-sponsored retreats or conferences
- Vehicle rental for church travel
- Lodging for benevolent assistance
- Church-related seminars, workshops, and registration fees

Personal use of the church's credit card should be reimbursed before the payment due date by the officer and/or employee. Credit card use for church business should be a privilege and abuse should be grounds for removal of an officer and termination of an employee. A credit card acceptance agreement detailing authorized usage and procedures should be signed upon acceptance.

Reimbursements

Reimbursements of expenses should only be made if pre-approved or if in church emergency. (Situation) In either

Managing with Ministry Excellence

case, proper receipt for the expense should be submitted for reimbursement. Small expense reimbursements may be made from the petty cash fund. Other expense reimbursements should be made by a church check.

Cashing Personal Checks

The church should not cash personal checks. To discourage this practice, a sign could be posted in the finance office stating this fact. Persons requiring this service should be referred to a local bank's ATM machine. If the check is good, the ATM will release the funds. If the check is bad, it will not bounce on the church's account. Some churches even have ATM machines in their narthex.

At its discretion, the church may cash church-issued checks. For example: An evangelist has conducted a week of revival services and is compensated on Friday night after the service concludes. His airline flight is early Sunday and he asks if the church will cash his check as he has little funds on hand and it will be another week before he returns home to deposit the check in his bank. There is no problem cashing the check for the evangelist.

How to handle gifts and bonuses that
are paid to board members

Gifts that are given to board members are taxable. Many churches are known to give small tokens of appreciation to their board members or church officers. Usually this is around the Christmas season. Needless to say, the receiver of the gift must report it as income. If the gift is valued ay $600 or more the church will need to issue a 1099-Misc form.

The person who receives the gift has one of two options to report it. It can be filled in on line 21 of the 1040 form and on the schedule SE form. The other way is to report it on a Schedule C and take deductions for any unreimbursed expenses.

Managing with Ministry Excellence

What to do when you pay a guest speaker cash?
**MOST CHURCHES ARE IN VIOLATION OF IRS
CODE WHEN THEY PAY CASH.** Unless there are things in order to create a paper trail, cash payments violate several sections of the IRS code. All money given to guest minister's should be reportable. These violations could cause the church penalties and charges against the board if applicable knowledge is present. Although it is not recommended, should your church have no other options but to give a guest minister cash, here are the following steps:

1. After counting the cash and making proper records, prepare a deposit form to be used for recording it into the petty cash fund
2. File the deposit into the petty cash fund as month received, be sure to document what the funds where received for
3. Then make note of the cash transaction debit for the amount given to the minister. Be sure to detail the

cash given to the minister was for religious services performed as wages for self-employed purposes.

4. Record all paperwork accordingly, if necessary ensure the minister fills out a 1099-Misc form

.

What occurs in the event of benevolence? Does the church need to issue a 1099-Misc to persons receiving benevolence over $600?

The IRS has addressed this question and has determined that a form 1099 is not required when giving benevolence because they are in essence substantial gifts and fall in the parameters of being exempt.

Be sure your church has a benevolence fund policy

The IRS has become more sensitive about churches establishing benevolence policies. The concern is the amounts of cash that are being paid directly to individuals in need. The IRS would prefer policies in place that would ensure objectivity. Your church needs to understand and identify their benevolence programs as pure acts of kindness. It is important you church develop a system where those in need do not become dependent on the benevolence. Be aware there are connivers and con artists who seek to take advantage of benevolence programs. With that being said, ensure your church has a system, requirements and policies in place that will identify those who are in need and filter out those who seek to take advantage of the system.

Because of the current economy there has been more people in need of church benevolence in recorded history. The IRS has set regulations in place that will allow churches to restrict their benevolence to members. Although, the Body of Christ has been commissioned to serve all be sure to use discernment when deciding this policy.

Who gets and who doesn't?
The IRS has put in place two regulations to help determine who should receive benevolence:

1. Income Tax Regulation 1.501(c)(3)-1(d)(2) says, "that person who are financially unable to care for themselves as a result of sudden and severe or overwhelming financial burdens arising from events beyond their control are proper objects of charity because they are considered to be "distressed".

2. Income Tax Regulation 1.170A(b)(2)(ii)(D) says, "a person who lacks the necessities of life, involving physical, mental, or emotional well-being as a result of poverty or temporary distress.

These statements can help in determining who qualifies for your church benevolence.

Confidentiality

Create something in your policy and requirements which state the person cannot make public the dollar amount they receive or for what purpose. If they would like to share of the great service, they can mention their need being met.

Managing with Ministry Excellence

Recommendations for creating a
Biblical benevolence policy

1. Form a group of persons chosen by the pastor or church leaders to be the committee that will create the policy, requirements and application for those seeking help

2. After prayer and deliberation the committee will submit their recommendations to the church leaders for consideration.

3. A church leadership meeting is to be convened in order to pass, or make suggestions to the committee, the proposed policy.

Proper benevolence documentation

1. All gifts given are given on a charitable basis and is for the purpose of advancing the church ministry.

2. Keep a record of names and addresses of those who have been given benevolence; record keeping is important.

3. The amount given to the individual and the purpose the funds were requested for.

4. The documented policy that determined specifically how the person was selected.

5. The relationship, if any, the recipient has to the church and its board of directors and executive leadership.

6. Any information you think necessary if the IRS were to request it.

*We write checks ONLY to the agency (power company, water company, mortgage company etc.) and not directly to the individual who is asking for assistance.

The Basics every benevolence policy should entail

1. The purpose for the benevolence program

2. Objective requirements that will identify persons who qualify

3. A person or group of persons responsible for approving applications

4. A policy for the maximum amount that can be given without board approval.

Managing with Ministry Excellence

How to record your benevolence distributions

It is a good practice to keep a record of these transactions on file for a minimum of 7 years. Keep the following:

1. The original application with documentation showing who approved it
2. The purpose the gift was given and to show the person qualified according to the church requirements
3. Documentation of the recipient's relationship with the church and board members
4. Noted approval by person responsible for the program

Church Credit Card Policy

Technology has afforded ministries the opportunity to manage funds by way of debit and credit cards. This convenience allows staff, pastor, administrator and even volunteers to make necessary purchases in order to support the daily operations of the ministry. Having this technology allows for convenience for the ministry and limits other paperwork and processes associated with reimbursing venders for services or products. My recommendation is

146

every church adopt a credit card policy. I have created a sample below for recommendation.

Credit Card Policy Example

- Church administrator or church treasurer has the authority to permit pastor, staff member, or church volunteer to use church credit card after purpose as been properly solidified.

- The credit card can only be used for purchases that support the ministry of the church.

- Sale receipts will be returned to the church treasurer, along with documented purpose for which the funds were used.

- If necessary, a detailed report of cost and items purchased should be provided and usage explained.

- Any personal expenditures created by pastor or staff will be documented as a personal expenditure and deducted from his or her paycheck.

Managing with Ministry Excellence

Accepting offerings and tithes by way of credit cards

Many church members prefer to the convenience of giving to the church by using their credit or debit cards. Receiving personal benefits in the process, like frequent flyer miles, the church does have to do its part in order to secure these payments. Credit card payments are safe, secure and are easier to accept for churches than cash and checks! If your church does not have a system in place to accept credit card payments, we would highly recommend this. There are three methods you can consider to implement this:

1. Include a position on the church envelope
2. Create opportunities for online giving
3. Kiosks are available for churches to place conveniently around the church campus.

Should the church establish credit?

In our opinion, Yes! Many churches and pastors have debated whether or not churches should establish lines of credit. We have seen in my personal church's ministry that having established credit in today's market opens economic opportunities for your church or ministry. Some churches see it as being unimportant. Our only consideration for them is to think what banks reference when applying for a loan. If you assume your church will acquire property, vehicles, or make other large purchases in the future, I think it a great idea to establish credit in the name of the church. Having good credit as a church will open opportunities for the church to easily secure items that will advance the ministry. Think about it in these terms: if you are able to acquire items that will advance the church, the ministry will grow as a whole. As numbers in membership increases, so will the possibility for giving.

The days of fundraising are over. There was a time when churches would host events, sell products, or solicit extra giving from its members in order to acquire products. Many churches have done away with this policy and have employed credit as a source of purchasing items that cannot be secured through the current church capital.

Managing with Ministry Excellence

Just as an individual uses credit wisely so should the church. Do not carry large balances. Do not spend unwisely. Pay balances off in a timely manner and be sure your church is registered with all eligible credit bureaus.:

Dun & Bradstreet

www.dnb.com

Experian Business

www.experian.com.business_services/index.html

Equifax Business

www.equifax.com/biz.index.shtml

Business Credit USA

www.businesscreditusa.com

Internet Resources:

Corporate forms and resolutions: http://www.amazon.com/Corporate-Forms-Kit-Rev-disk/dp/1574100572#reader_1574100572

Church Tax Laws: www.churchlawandtax.com/aboutus.php

Church Accounting and Taxes: www.chitwoods.com

Church Business Administration, Salary, Survey Etc.: www.nacba.net/Pages/Home.aspx

Church Staffing Resource and Job Descriptions: www.ChurchStaffing.com

IRS Forms: www.irs.gov/formspubs/

Church Forms:

www.friezconsulting.com/index.php?option=com_content&task=view&i

Sample Cash Collection Form

CASH COLLECTION FORM

Please do not hold cash or checks. All cash should be turned in weekly by each Sunday.

Date: _____   Activity: _____

Ministry/Dept.: _____   Signature: _____

Completed by: _____   Signature: _____
(Print Name)

CASH			CHECKS		
	Quantity	$ Amount	Name		Check #
100's				$	
50's				$	
20's				$	
10's				$	
5's				$	
1's				$	
Quarters				$	
Dimes				$	
Nickels				$	
Pennies				$	
TOTAL CASH			TOTAL CHECKS	$	
				$	

List of Individuals with Cash Donations	Amount
	$
	$
	$
	$
	$
	$
	$
	$
	$
Amount from attached list (if applicable)	$
Total Cash from Individuals	$

TOTAL CASH $ _____

TOTAL CHECKS $ _____

Less: Start up Cash Change $ _____

GROSS DEPOSIT $ _____

Submitted by: _____
Print Name:

Funds Received by: _____
Church Administrator's Office

Funds Verified by: _____
Finance Room/Print Name:
Date: _____

Managing with Ministry Excellence

Sample Copy Request Form

COPY REQUEST FORM

Today's Date : _____

Ministry _____

Account # _____

Submitted By _____

Phone No. _____

Date and Time Needed _____

Number of Originals _____

Number of Copies _____

One-sided ____
Two-sided ____

		SPECIAL INSTRUCTIONS
Collated	____	
Grouped	____	
Stapled	____	
Book Style	____	
Color Copies	____	
Color Paper	____	
3 Holed Punch	____	
Comb Bound	____	

Return to _____ Phone No. _____

Office Hours   9:00am to 4:00pm   Monday thru Friday

Thank you for your cooperation.
The Church Staff   Completed_____

PLEASE COMPLETE THIS FORM AND RETURN TO CHURCH ADMINISTRATOR 7 DAYS IN ADVANCE OF DATE NEEDED. THIS WILL PROVIDE SUFFICIENT TIME TO COORDINATE AND COMPLETE YOUR REQUEST. BE MINDFUL THAT IF THIS FORM IS NOT RETURNED IN A TIMELY MANNER THAT THERE IS NO GUARANTEE THAT YOU WILL HAVE THE COPIES YOU NEED.

Managing with Ministry Excellence

Sample Van Request Form

VAN REQUEST FORM

Ministry/Auxiliary _____

Date of road trip _____

Destination of road trip _____

Contact Person _____
(Secretary of Auxiliary or designated driver)

Number of passengers_____   Time of departure _____

Report time _____   Number of days _____

Purpose of trip _____
_____

Special Instructions:
_____
_____
_____

President of Ministry/Auxiliary _____

Request Forms should be submitted to the Special Projects Coordinator a minimum of fourteen (14) business days prior to date van is needed.

Managing with Ministry Excellence

Sample Room Request Form

Room Reservation Request Form

Today's Date _____

Ministry/Auxiliary _____

Date of request _____   Time _____

Contact Person(s) _____

Phone _____

Description of event _____

_____

Room arrangement request _____

_____

_____

Location desired _____

Number of attendees _____

Signature _____

****

Room assigned _____

Program Office _____

Managing with Ministry Excellence

Sample Photography/ Video Request Form

PHOTOGRAPHY / VIDEO MINISTRY
REQUEST FORM

Date Received: _____

Ministry / Auxiliary Name: _____

Contact Name: _____   Phone: _____

Work: _____

Alternate Contact: _____   Phone: _____

Services Needed: ____ Photos

____ Portraits

____ Video

Date Services needed: _____

Times services needed: _____

Location required for services _____

Occasion: _____

(Example: Retreats, Banquets, Breakfast, Femart, Weddings, Funerals, Lock-ins, Get-Away, Baby Dedications, Anniversaries, Special Events, and Receptions, etc.)

Type of film: ____ Color

(Takes one (1) week to develop.)

____ Black & White

LOCATION ASSIGNED FOR PROJECT: _____

ALL REQUEST MUST BE SUBMITTED ONE (1) MONTH IN ADVANCE TO THE PROGRAM AND FACILITY COODINATOR.

Date Assigned _____

Managing with Ministry Excellence

Sample Dance Ministry Request Form

Ministry Name _____

Contact Person _____

Telephone _____   Email _____

Event _____   Date _____

Time _____   Location _____

Place a check next to the group requested to dance in ministry:

Children Ages 5-7 ____

Youth Ages 12-17 ____

Adults 18 - Over ____

Soloist ____   Praise Dance ____

Event Colors _____

Stage: Yes ____   No ____

Practice site available: Yes ____   No ____

Rehearsal Date _____

Additional Information: _____

_____

_____

_____

_____

Managing with Ministry Excellence

Sample Prayer Request Form

PRAYER REQUEST / PRAISE REPORT

"Be anxious for nothing, but in everything by prayer and supplication, with thanksgiving, let your requests be made known to God; and the peace of God, which surpasses all understanding, will guard your hearts and minds through Christ Jesus." (Philippians 4: 6-7)

Please check one:
☐ *Please pray for*   ☐ *Praise Report for*

Name: _____   Date: _____

Address: _____   Check one:

City / State / Zip _____   ☐ New prayer request
☐ Update to previous prayer request

Is this person a member of The GPGBC? ☐ *Yes* ☐ *No* ☐ *Not sure*   ☐ Praise report of previous request

Is this person a Christian? ☐ *Yes* ☐ *No* ☐ *Not sure*

Can praise report be share to exhort the church body? ☐ *Yes* ☐ *No*

_____

_____

_____

Person making request: Is this person making the request a member of The GPGBC? ☐ *Yes* ☐ *No*

Name: _____

Address: _____

City: _____   State: _____   Zip: _____

Phone: (h) _____   (w) _____

Relationship to person prayed for:
☐ *Self*   ☐ *Family Member*   ☐ *Friend*   ☐ *Other*

This form has been distributed to:

_____   _____

_____   _____

by: *(Initials of person completing form)*

Sample Death and Bereavement Form

Death - Bereavement Form

Date _____ Time (:) Called received by: _____

Caller Name _____ Relation to Deceased _____ Telephone No. _____

Card(s) Sent ☐ Flowers Ordered ☐   Date Ordered: _____

Contact Telephone Numbers

Contact Name _____

Deceased Information ☐ Member ☐ Non-Member

Home No. _____
Work No. _____

Name _____ Other Contact No. _____

Home Address _____

Mortuary Information

Name _____ Telephone No. _____

Mortuary Address _____

Funeral Services Information (i.e., Church)

Name of Facility _____

Facility Address _____

Wake: Yes ☐ No ☐ Wake Location: _____

Managing with Ministry Excellence

Sample Vehicle Checklist Form

river's Last Name _____ Driver's First Name _____
Please PRINT

ate: _____ Time in _____ (AM/PM) Time out _____ (AM\PM)

estination _____

ehicle Used	Milege Out	Milege In
Van		
15 Passenger		
25 Passenger		

>proximately Gas Reading
as Out   Full   3/4   1/2   1/4   E   Gas In   Full   3/4   1/2   1/4   E

EXTERIOR INSPECTION
Place an (✓) mark in each box to indicate inspection is complete.
Place an (x) mark to indicate a problem with vehicle.

OUT	IN	ITEM	OUT	IN	ITEM
		Front Left Tire/ Hubcap/Lugs			Right Rear Tire/Hubcap/Lugs
		Door			Doors/Body
		Mirror			Mirror
		Rear Left Tire			Front Right Tire/Hubcap/Lug
		Rear Bumper			Front Bumper
		Tail Lights			Head Lights
		Tag			Fluid Leaks
		Doors			Wiper Blades
		Other			Other

Give Brief Damage Description _____

_____

OUT	IN	INTERIOR	OUT	IN	INTERIOR
		Dash Fluid Gauges			Seat belts
		Head Lighting			Paper/Debris
		Floor			Spills/Odor

Give Brief Description (other) _____

_____

_____

Managing with Ministry Excellence

{CHURCH NAME}
FINANCE OFFICE - SAMPLE COUNT SHEET

SPEAKER: _____

SERVICE: ☐ A.M.   ☐ REVIVAL   DAY: _____

☐ P.M.   ☐ MUSICAL   DATE: _____

☐ MID-WEEK   ☐ OTHER: _____

☐ TITHES ☐ OFFERINGS ☐ BUILDING FUND ☐ MISSIONS ☐ BENEVOLENCE ☐ OTHER: _____

A) CASH	AMT.		B) STRAPS	NO.		AMT.
100's	$_____		$2000 x	_____	= $	_____
50's	_____		1000 x	_____	=	_____
20's	_____		500 x	_____	=	_____
10's	_____		250 x	_____	=	_____
5's	_____		200 x	_____	=	_____
2's	_____		100 x	_____	=	_____
1's	_____		50 x	_____	=	_____
			Loose Cash		=	_____
(1) SUB-TOTAL	$_____		(1) SUB-TOTAL			$_____

COINS	AMT.		ROLLED COINS	NO.		AMT.
Dollars	$_____		$10.00 x	_____	= $	_____
Half-Dollars	_____		5.00 x	_____	=	_____
Quarters	_____		2.50 x	_____	=	_____
Dimes	_____		.50 x	_____	=	_____
Nickels	_____		_____ x	_____	=	_____
Pennies	_____		Loose Coins		=	_____
(2) SUB-TOTAL	$_____		(2) SUB-TOTAL			$_____
(3) CHECKS	$_____		(3) CHECKS			$_____
TOTALS A (1+2+3)	$_____		TOTALS B (1+2+3)			$_____

TOTAL TO BE DEPOSITED IN BANK AND VERIFIED BY BANK DEPOSIT SLIP

COUNTERS SIGNATURE(S): _____

_____

_____

SAMPLE LETTER

**"Notification to Minister of
Housing Allowance by the Church"**

DATE

Reverend John Doe, Pastor
Heavenly Host Church
333 Beinformed Way
Anywhere, GA 38333

RE: Notification by Employer

Dear

This is to advise you that the meeting of the Board of Trustees of _____
_____was held on _____ in
reference to your parsonage allowance for the year _____. **The board officials
designated and fixed the amount of $_____as your salary.**

Accordingly, $_____ of the total payment to you during the _____year will
constitute parsonage allowance and the balance will constitute compensation under **Section
107 of the Internal Revenue Code which states that a minister is allowed to exclude
from gross income the rental allowance paid as part of rental compensation to rent or
provide a home.**

You should keep an accurate record of your expenditures to rent or provide a home in order
to be able to substantiate any amount excluded from gross income in filing your Federal
Income Tax Return.

Sincerely,

Managing with Ministry Excellence

Church Organizational Chart

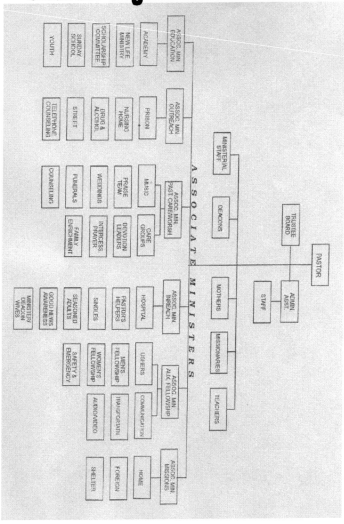

Sample Floral Request Form

Receiver: _____

Deliver to:

Hospital : _____

_____

_____

Funeral : _____
Home   _____

_____

Home :   _____

_____

_____

Managing with Ministry Excellence

Sample Benevolent Assistance Application

Social Security No.: _____   Spouse's Social Security No.: _____

Date: _____   ☐ Own   ☐ Rent   ☐ Other _____

Name: _____   Phone ( ) _____

Address: _____

City: _____   State: _____   Zipcode: _____

Age: _____   ☐ Single   ☐ Married   ☐ Divorced   ☐ Separated   ☐ Widow

Spouse's Name: _____   Spouse's Employment: _____

Children's Ages: _____

Needs: ☐ Food   ☐ Clothing   ☐ Shelter   ☐ Rent / Mortgage   ☐ Utilities _____

☐ Transient   ☐ Other (Explain) _____

Deadline: _____   Amount Needed: $ _____

Have you been helped previously by this Church?   ☐ Yes   ☐ No

What did you receive? _____   When? _____

Others organizations you have applied to for this need? _____

_____

Please explain the circumstances which brought about this need. _____

_____

_____

_____

Home Church: _____   Phone ( ) _____

Church Address: _____

Pastor's Name: _____   Phone ( ) _____

Doctor's Name: _____   Phone ( ) _____

Landlord's Name: _____   Phone ( ) _____

Landlord's Address: _____

Monthly Average Cost: Mortgage/Rent $ _____   Auto $ _____   Electric $ _____

Water $ _____   Phone $ _____   Medical $ _____   Gas $ _____

164

ALL ARISE: CHURCH ADMINISTRATION

Managing with Ministry Excellence

Other (Explain) _____

If you are requesting a bill payment, please supply the following information. (For more than one bill, please attach the additional information)

Company Name: _____

Phone ( ) _____ Contact Person: _____

Address: _____

City _____ State: _____ Zip Code: _____

Account Number: _____ Total Amount Due $ _____

Amount Required $ _____

List Two Personal References:

Name: _____ Phone ( ) _____

Address: _____

City _____ State _____ Zip Code: _____

Name: _____ Phone ( ) _____

Address: _____

City _____ State _____ Zip Code _____

Other Sources Willing to Assist with this Need:

Name: _____ Phone ( ) _____ Amount $ ____

Name: _____ Phone ( ) _____ Amount $ ____

Name: _____ Phone ( ) _____ Amount $ ____

Do Not Write Below This Line – For Church Use Only

Date Application Received in this Office: _____

Information from Community Help Line (Contact Name) _____

Disapproved ____ Reason: _____

Approved ____ Approved by: _____

Date Paid: _____ Amount $ _____ Check No. _____

Written by: _____ Payable to: _____

Send to: _____

Address: _____

City _____ State _____ Zip Code: _____

Comments: _____

Signatures: (At Least Two Committee Members or One Member and Pastor)

_____

165

Managing with Ministry Excellence

Sample Church Property Request Form

Furniture/Equipment Loan Authorization

Permission is hereby granted to (name) _____

to borrow (list item(s)) _____

_____

_____

Model No. (if applicable): _____

_____

_____

Serial No. (if applicable): _____

_____

_____

The above items to be returned and checked in on (date) _____

_____   _____
James D. McWhorter, Church Administrator   Signature of Borrower

_____   _____
Maintenance Personnel (Checked Out)   Name of Borrower (Please Print)

_____   _____
Date   Borrower's Phone Number or Cell Phone Number

_____   _____
Maintenance Personnel (Checked In)   Date

_____
Date

Managing with Ministry Excellence

Sample Special Items Order Form

Date of Request _____

Ministry _____

Ordered By _____

Vendor _____ Budget Line No. _____

Qty.	Catalog Page No.	Item No.	Description	Unit Price	Total Price

TOTAL (This page.) $_____

Approved By _____ Date _____

Managing with Ministry Excellence

About the Authors

Dr. William E. Flippin, Sr. is a native of Nashville, Tennessee. Dr. Flippin has earned a Bachelor of Arts degree in Mathematics and Business Administration from Fisk University in Nashville, Tennessee. In addition, Dr. Flippin holds a Master of Divinity (Cum Laude) from Candler School of Theology at Emory University in Atlanta, Georgia. Dr. Flippin earned a Doctorate of Ministry from McCormick Theological Seminary in Chicago, Illinois. Dr. Flippin is currently a Certified Life Transformational Coach and also a Certified Leadership Coach Trainer where his main objective is to *raise leaders*. Currently, he faithfully serves as Senior Pastor of The Greater Piney Grove Baptist Church ("The Grove") in Atlanta, Georgia. Since 1990, Pastor Flippin has led The Greater Piney Grove to a unique sense of mission and outreach. Recently, "The Grove" purchased 22-additional acres on their church property to secure a total of 50 acres which is named The Promise Land at Eastlake.

He also serves as the Founder and CEO of The Flippin Legacy Ministries, Inc, The Pearl Initiative, Inc. (Non-Profit); and Pearls of Great Price Ministries, Inc (For-Profit). He is the author of five books: In My Father's House, Order in the Church, Order in the Pulpit, God's Order, Vision 20/20. Dr. Flippin has been married for over thirty-seven years to Sylvia Taylor Flippin, who is an instructional coach for the DeKalb County Board of Education. Dr. and Mrs. Flippin are the proud parents of one daughter, Miss Sylvia Joi, and three sons who continue the family legacy of preaching: William E. Flippin, Jr. (Kedra S.), Richard C. Flippin, Joseph C. T. Flippin (Kendall D.) Flippin

Managing with Ministry Excellence

James D. McWhorter serves as the current church administrator of The Greater Piney Grove Baptist Church and has served formerly at Cathedral of Faith Church of God in Christ, both in Atlanta, GA, serving in this capacity for over 32 years. He has conducted numerous seminars and workshops to train and equip church leaders and laity in various aspects of church administration, staffing, stewardship, and financial integrity. He has also been privileged to minister and train pastors and church leaders in Kenya, East Africa and Ghana and Nigeria, West Africa.

He and his wife of 41 years are the proud parents of three children, James III, Eric and Camille and five grandchildren.

Other Reading Material

God's Order: Order in the Church

God's Order: Order in the Pulpit

20/20 Vision for the Victor

All can be purchased at Amazon.com